Guide for
Alternate Route Teachers

Second Edition

Guide for Alternate Route Teachers

Strategies for Literacy Development, Classroom Management, and Teaching and Learning, K–12

Frances A. Levin
New Jersey City University

Mary Alice McCullough
New Jersey City University

Boston   Columbus   Indianapolis   New York   San Francisco   Upper Saddle River
Amsterdam   Cape Town   Dubai   London   Madrid   Milan   Munich   Paris   Montreal   Toronto
Delhi   Mexico City   Sao Paulo   Sydney   Hong Kong   Seoul   Singapore   Taipei   Tokyo

For Amanda and Addison, who remind me each day of the wonder and joy that learning brings to our lives. —M.A.M.

This book is dedicated to my supportive and wonderful family. First, to my loving parents, Laura and Morris Silbereich, who taught me how to be a teacher at a very young age. Next, to my husband, Harry, for his love and ongoing interest and support of my work for the past 35 years. Finally, to my greatest accomplishments, Jessica and Jared, who have always provided unending love and joy to me. —F.L.

Vice President and Editor-in-Chief: Aurora Martínez Ramos
Editor: Erin K. L. Grelak
Editorial Assistant: Michelle Hochberg
Executive Marketing Manager: Krista Clark
Production Editor: Janet Domingo
Editorial Production Service: Element LLC
Manufacturing Buyer: Megan Cochran
Interior and Electronic Composition: Element LLC
Cover Designer: Linda Knowles

Library of Congress Cataloging-in-Publication Data
Levin, Frances A.
    Guide for alternate route teachers : strategies for literacy development, classroom management, and teaching and learning, K-12 / Frances A. Levin, Mary Alice McCullough. — 2nd ed.
        p. cm.
    Includes index.
    ISBN 978-0-13-231637-8
1. First year teachers. 2. Teachers—Professional relationships. 3. Teachers—Certification. 4. Classroom management. 5. Language arts. I. McCullough, Mary Alice. II. Title.
LB2844.1.N4L48 2012
371.102—dc22

2011004911

Printed in the United States of America

10 9 8 7 6 5 4 3 2 1   15 14 13 12 11

www.pearsonhighered.com

ISBN-10:   0-13-231637-4
ISBN-13: 978-0-13-231637-8

Contents

List of Models

Preface

Since its inception, the Alternate Route Certification Process has helped thousands of men and women throughout the United States enter the teaching profession. This process allows degreed professionals with strong content area backgrounds and relevant work experience to begin teaching prior to completing the preparatory courses in educational methodology, theory, and pedagogy that are required of all teachers seeking permanent certification.

We wrote this book with the intention of providing valuable information, models, and resources to help guide these professionals and their decision making as they transition into their new roles as teachers. This guide is not intended to be used as a primary textbook. Its purpose is to bridge the alternate route teachers' existing information gap *as* they complete their required teacher education training. Our hope is that teachers will see this guide as a valuable resource that they can turn to to find quick solutions and understandings that they can immediately apply to their classroom practices.

The topics in this book address the issues that have the most immediate concern for new teachers, such as teacher expectations, classroom management, assessment, unit and lesson design, and so on. Chapter 5, "Literacy Instruction K–12" and Chapter 6, "Literacy across the Curriculum," are specifically dedicated to literacy development. Chapter 7, "Helping All Students Find Success" focuses on the specific challenges faced by English Language Learners, struggling readers, gifted readers, and students with special needs. We felt these chapters were important to include because literacy skills (reading, writing, interpreting, viewing, speaking, and critical thinking) play a major role in advancing student learning in *all* grades and in *all* content areas. For this reason, we chose examples to further clarify the strategies and methodologies in this book primarily from the language arts. Our thinking and hope was that future teachers would have a strong understanding of literacy, which would enable them to accommodate the procedures and strategies to their own content areas.

This book further supports teachers' understandings by providing relevant research and by placing the major educational issues with which they will be confronted within their historical contects. In addition, we provide lists of websites and texts that teachers can access to broaden their scope and knowledge base.

Although the chapters in this book can be read sequentially, they need not be. Each is a self-contained body of information with references, when needed, to related information in other chapters. In addition, although this guide was written as a support for alternate route teachers, it was purposely penned for the students of these teachers who we see as the ultimate beneficiaries of their teaching success.

New to This Edition

Because so many new and pre-service teachers found this guide to be a valuable resource, we were asked to collaborate on a second edition. We based the revisions in this edition on direct feedback from alternate route teachers and their instructors. Teachers indicated that they needed more strategies for introducing and integrating technology and for dealing with learners who had academic needs beyond the scope of regular classroom teaching and learning (English Language Learners, struggling readers, gifted readers, and students with special needs). In response, we have significantly revised Chapter 7, "Helping All Students Find Success" by adding recommendations and more research-based strategies to address all three of these issues. We also added a new chapter, Chapter 8, "Using Technology to Support Literacy Instruction: Getting Started." This chapter focuses on specific strategies teachers new to technology can use to introduce and integrate technology, beginning with computers, into their teaching practices. Other changes to this edition include:

■ **Greater Focus on Supporting Literacy Instruction**
This new edition focuses on elementary as well as secondary literacy instruction. By also including very specific information on a variety of learners, we have provided the information that every teacher needs in order to encourage improvements in literacy. English Language Learners, struggling readers, and students with special needs are a considerable force in our schools and teachers must understand how to work effectively with all students.

■ **Chapter 2: Classroom Management**
This chapter was revised to include 40% updated resources and the addition of a section on Online Resources.

■ **Chapter 3: Planning for Success: Unit and Lesson Planning and Design**
This chapter was revised to include the addition of a section on Online Resources.

■ Chapter 4: Evaluating Student Knowledge and Performance

This chapter was revised to include 40% updated resources and the addition of a section on Online Resources.

■ Chapter 5: Literacy Instruction K–12

This chapter was revised to incorporate additional information designed to help secondary school teachers who are faced with students who have difficulty reading the material. Information in this chapter provides strategies, recommendations, and explanations that offer assistance to teachers. There are also 33% new and updated references plus the addition of a section on Online Resources.

■ Chapter 6: Literacy across the Curriculum

This chapter was revised to include updated references and research and more online resources. Reviewing new research and updating references assures teachers that they are reading the most relevant information available.

■ Chapter 7: Helping All Students Find Success: Working with English Language Learners, Struggling Readers, Gifted Readers, and Students with Special Needs

This chapter was significantly revised to add new information on English Language Learners, struggling readers, gifted readers, and students with special needs. Since these students often present unique challenges to new teachers, this chapter was revised to incorporate foundational information and practical classroom recommendations that will help alternate route teachers understand how to work with all students. References have also been updated and we have added a section on Online Resources.

■ Chapter 8: Using Technology to Support Literacy Instruction: Getting Started

This chapter is new to the guide. Included in this new chapter: a rationale for integrating technology and literacy teaching and learning, policies for Internet use, strategies for ensuring student safety on the Internet, strategies for ensuring teaching suggestions (K–12), 38 websites, online and print resources, and advice from the field.

■ Chapter 9: The Home-School Connection

Parent involvement is such a critical component of student success that we provided online resources and updated references for teachers who want to understand and be proactive toward the families of their students.

Acknowledgments

Special thanks to my assistant, Pat Shinners, for her technological expertise and overall assistance for the past 15 years. Thank you to the thousands of alternate route teachers in the New Pathways to Teaching in New Jersey program who completed surveys, offered advice, and provided the inspiration for this book. Their needs and feedback have become the foundation for the Second Edition. Kudos to our editors, Aurora Martínez Ramos and Erin Grelak, for their kindness and support throughout this process. Their recognition of the contributions and importance of alternate route teachers has made a significant difference. —F.L.

My special thanks to Mr. Medica and his sixth-grade class at Egg Harbor Township Intermediate School who charmed me with their fascination with Roman culture and allowed me to photograph them in the act of learning. My thanks also go to Sally Dunn and Marci Grabelle for their valuable advice and counsel. Thanks to John Scharff and John Sciarappa and their students at Freehold Township High School for inviting me into their classrooms and permitting me to use their photographs in this book. I would like to also express my gratitude to my husband, Bruce, who gave me the guidance and inspiration to complete this project. My final thanks go to our editors, Aurora Martínez Ramos and Erin Grelak, whose valuable advice and counsel brought this book to life. —M.A.M.

Special thanks to those who made comments on the manuscript: Joseph G. Polvere, University Alternate Route Program based at Bergen Community College; Sherry Sanden, Washington State University; and Barbara Stanley, Valdosa State University.

What Are the Expectations for Teachers in Today's Schools?

Making a life change can be at once exciting and exhilarating and daunting and exhausting. Knowing in advance what will be expected of you will lessen the anxiety and confirm that your decision to enter the field of education is a good one for you. A good place to begin is with a cursory glance at teacher expectations and how they have changed over the years.

Changes in Teacher Expectations

Teaching and learning have changed radically over the past forty years. At one time, teaching expectations were limited to presenting lessons and grading papers. Preparation was minimal because programmed lessons with answer keys and objective tests

were purchased along with the textbooks, making it possible for teachers to easily satisfy their responsibilities during their contractual nine-to-three workday. Classroom discipline was generally not a problem because teachers had both parental and administrative support. Most students actually feared a trip to the principal's office because of the additional consequences they knew they would face once they got home. Curriculum and standards were determined by local boards of education, and accountability rarely went beyond the building level. This, you will find, has all changed.

A major change is in the academic, performance, and professional expectations for teachers. Research in teaching and learning, technology, and globalization has changed the face of teaching. The responsibilities of teachers and administrators continue to increase exponentially in an effort to keep up with the ever-growing internal and external demands placed on schools. Unlike educators in the past, teachers today have as their primary responsibility to prepare their students with the skills, concepts, and knowledge base that will enable them to compete in a demanding global environment that requires that they not only *know more* but also be able to *apply what they know* to the unknown. To accomplish this, teachers are being asked to introduce curricular skills and concepts much earlier and in much more depth. Consequently, young children are starting to learn how to read and write in preschool; middle school students are taking algebra and biology; and high school students are taking college-level classes for credit. These curricular demands require that teachers themselves have not only a strong content area background but also a strong knowledge base in teaching pedagogy that would enable them to teach students in a way that would maximize their understanding and ability to apply what they have been taught.

Another change is society's expectation of who should be taught. Until the middle of the twentieth century, the focus of the school's attention was on the academic preparation of those entering the professional fields. Advanced courses such as foreign languages, abstract math, chemistry, and physics were exclusively reserved for those who were college bound. The other students were given general courses such as applied math, nonacademic English, and earth science, which did not require students to go beyond literal understandings of the texts they were reading. These students, most of whom entered the workforce right after graduating from high school, were being prepared for jobs that were characteristically regimented and systematic. The advent of computers changed all of that. Not only did computers change the way we communicated with each other, they also changed the way goods and services were produced, marketed, and delivered. This new technology began to rapidly replace unskilled laborers, forcing millions to be reeducated in order to compete for jobs. Today's jobs and the jobs of the future require that employees have advanced technological skills and the ability to think critically and develop new ways to use those skills. For example, auto mechanics today must be technologically savvy to be able to diagnose and solve problems embedded in an automobile's complex computer systems. This shift in technology has had a tremendous impact on schools and teachers, who, seemingly overnight, have become responsible for preparing *all* students—not just a select few—to think critically. This was the impetus for radical changes in curriculum and required that the doors to those advanced courses, focusing on critical thinking as well as on content, be opened to all students. Within a short period of time, this drive to educate all of our students with the same advanced skills and concepts had gone beyond the social implications to become a national economic imperative. To ensure that all students were being given the skills and concepts they needed, state and national standards were set and tests were developed to measure attainment of those standards. This change in focus had a tremendous impact on teacher expectations. Teachers are now not only expected to teach the content and skills identified by the standards, they are also being held accountable for their students' mastery of those skills and concepts.

A final change in teacher responsibilities happened as a result of the vast amount of research that has been done in the areas of teaching and learning. For a long time, students were taught with methods based on the stimulus-response-reinforcement learning theories posed by Skinner's (1974) research with animals. The problem with this method is that it trained students, like animals, to respond to, not to think or be able to generalize information in other areas of their lives. Thanks to the researchers and scholars who have followed Skinner, we now know a great deal more about how students learn and what strategies teachers can use to maximize their students' learning. We know, for example, that:

- Children learn at higher levels and at greater rates when they are actively engaged in their own learning (Piaget, 1995; Vygotsky, 1986).

- Comprehension is increased significantly if students are given problems to solve and the opportunity to use talk to negotiate meaning to solve those problems (Reader-Response Theory) (Beach 1993; McCullough 2002; Rosenblatt, 1976; Vygotsky, 1986).

- Tracking doesn't work. Children who are tracked into remedial classes rarely advance to the next level (Gamoran, 1986; Goodlad, 1984; Wheelock, 1992).

- Teaching vocabulary with lists without multiple opportunities to use the words in different contexts doesn't work. Students learn best when given multiple contextual strategies, for example, clustering (Marzano & Marzano, 1988), word mapping (Blanchowicz, 1986), collaborative word selection (Fisher, Blanchowicz, & Smith, 1991), and word play (Nagy & Scott, 2001).

- Children will read if they are given texts that interest them (Harkrader & Moore, 1997; Huck & Kuhn, 1968).

- Comprehension and retention are increased significantly if students are given opportunities to make connections and apply what they know to their own lives (Rosenblatt, 1976).

- Just because children can read words with accuracy and fluency doesn't mean they understand what they are reading (Allington & Cunningham, 2002).

- A child's literacy development is enhanced significantly when taught with a balanced approach to literacy instruction (Clay, 1985; Strickland, Galda, & Cullinan, 2004).

- Students learn best when their learning style matches their teacher's teaching style (Gardner, 1983).

- Student failures can be minimized when student weaknesses are identified prior to the failure with assessments that are varied, frequent, and ongoing (Clay, 1991; Galda, Cullinan, & Strickland, 1993).

Most important, current research continues to show that, although some people believe that quality education is in direct proportion to funding, the most important influence on student learning is not money or computers or even books; it's their teachers (Barnes, Britton, & Torbe, 1989; Fish, 1980; McCullough, 2002). For this reason, teachers today have the responsibility, expectation, and moral obligation to provide their students with a quality education using strategies and methodologies that are grounded in scientifically based research.

What Do Administrators Expect of New Teachers?

Administrators, who are supported by content area supervisors, are primarily concerned with issues dealing with faculty, discipline, safety, and school operations. In addition, they are accountable to the state and to their local boards of education for their students meeting local, state, and national academic standards. Administrators (K–12) will expect new teachers to do the following:

- Come to school every day prepared to teach lessons that will prepare students to meet standards on state and national tests.

- Be punctual. (Report to school on time and remain in the building until the designated leaving time; arrive at classes, duties, and meetings on time, etc.)

- Present themselves as role models by dressing, speaking, and acting in a professional manner.

- Attend and participate meaningfully in monthly faculty meetings, Back-to-School Nights, parent-teacher conferences, and other events.

- Keep accurate and up-to-date academic and attendance records.

- Maintain a safe physical and emotional student environment both inside and outside the classroom, which includes protecting students from both physical attacks and verbal abuse as well as exposure to hazardous areas or substances.

- Maintain a neat, orderly, and inviting physical environment for students.

- Take charge of students during drills for fire, bomb threats, and terrorist attacks, which includes taking and reporting attendance.

- Maintain classroom discipline and decorum.

- Report suspected physical and/or psychological abuse of students.

- Enforce the school's discipline code and report infractions (e.g., drug and alcohol use, excessive tardiness, insubordination).

- Comply promptly with requests from parents, staff, or other administrators for information or reports.

- Submit grades and progress reports on time.

- Provide accommodations for students with special needs.

- Administer standardized tests.

- Report punctually to and supervise assigned duties (such as hall, cafeteria, bus, lavatory).

- Serve on special committees (i.e., discipline committee, Back-to-School Night committee, prom).

Note: Some administrators may expect that all new teachers will take on additional responsibilities such as coaching a sport or advising a club.

What Do Content Supervisors Expect of New Teachers?

Content area supervisors' concerns are primarily academic. They are responsible for ensuring that students receive a quality education and that teachers are given the support they need in the form of materials, equipment, mentoring, and professional development to make that happen. In return, content area supervisors will expect the following of new teachers:

- Be familiar with local, state, and national standards.

- Develop units of instruction using scientifically based teaching strategies that support local, state, and national standards.

- Be prepared every day to present lessons that are differentiated, student-centered, challenging, active, and interesting.

- Use teacher-developed assessments and standardized test results to inform instruction.

- Use ongoing and varied assessment tools to evaluate student learning.

- Be reflective practitioners who allot time each day to reflect, assess, and make necessary modifications to the day's activities (lessons; interactions with students, parents, and colleagues; new policies or procedures, etc.).

- Submit weekly detailed lesson plans in the required format.

- Design learning centers and bulletin board displays to support unit objectives (K–6).

- Work closely with the Child Study Team to develop lessons for students with special needs. The Child Study Team is a team of professionals who set and manage the educational and behavioral programs of students with disabilities.

- Attend and participate in a meaningful way in monthly department meetings.

- Submit written requests for books, materials, and supplies.

- Maintain accurate and up-to-date grade and attendance books.

- Keep parents informed of their child's progress via phone calls, email messages, newsletters, progress reports, or letters home.

- Serve on committees to develop curriculum and review new materials for possible purchase.

- Remain current by continuing personal professional development by taking graduate courses, attending professional meetings and conferences, participating in teacher mentoring programs, and so on.

- Be kept informed of both problems and successes that you are having.

Note: In smaller school districts, the roles of the building administrator and the content area supervisor are often assumed by the same person.

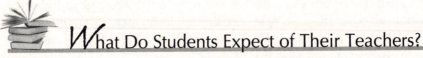

What Do Students Expect of Their Teachers?

Students, regardless of age or feigned indifference, come to school each day with high expectations of the teachers, who for many of them are the people with whom they spend the majority of their day. A sad reality is that some students have more contact hours with their teachers than with their own parents. This may account for the change over the years in what students expect from their teachers—from being primarily impersonal and academic to being more personal as well as academic. When asked, students responded that they expected the following of their teachers:

- Know who they are.
- Like them and like teaching.
- Come to class every day prepared to teach lessons in a way that is personable and understandable.
- Be knowledgeable, current, clear, concise, and consistent.
- Be approachable, flexible, and open to opposing ideas.
- Be good role models with a sense of humor.
- Be fair, encouraging, sensitive, and nonthreatening.
- Return work in a timely manner, preferably the next day.
- Be more than "correctors." Acknowledge the students for something done well.
- Maintain discipline in the classroom.
- Participate in school activities (coach, attend sporting events, buy fund-raising candy bars, etc.).
- Be available and genuinely willing to provide extra help or counseling when needed.
- Advocate for them when they have problems.
- Keep them safe from physical and psychological attacks.

What Do Parents Expect of Their Children's Teachers?

Because many students live in a single working-parent home or in a home where both parents work, there is an increasing demand on teachers' time. More and more, parents are expecting teachers to accept responsibilities that would have traditionally been theirs. Many schools have accommodated parental requests by expanding their curriculum to include courses in sex education, parenting skills, and values clarification with the expectation that teachers will teach them. In addition, parents expect teachers to do the following:

- Value and nurture their children.
- Have their children's best interests at the heart of each action and decision.
- Be competent, current, and effective.

- Teach the content needed for their children to succeed on standardized tests and in the classes that follow.

- Academically challenge their children with lessons that will move them beyond their current grade level.

- Be sensitive, understanding, and attentive to children's individual needs.

- Provide extra help when needed.

- Provide educational experiences beyond the classroom (class trips, guest speakers, etc.).

- Keep them informed (for example, through phone calls, email messages, notes home, progress reports).

- Be a positive role model.

- Keep their children safe from physical harm and from the potentially psychologically debilitating taunts of bullies.

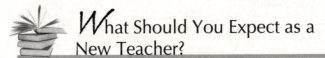 What Should You Expect as a New Teacher?

It's important that you not only have a good idea of what is expected of you as a first-year teacher, you should also have an idea of what it is that you should expect. Your list of first-year teacher expectations should include the following:

- A safe working environment.

- Administrative support. If you have a problem with a student or parent that you have been unable to handle on your own, you should expect intervention and backing from the administration in some form (such as conference, detention, letter home, suspension). You should also expect to be advised of the outcome of the intervention.

- Supervisory support. It is understood that no one comes to teaching fully prepared or equipped for the task. You should, therefore, expect ongoing support from your supervisor through frequent classroom observations and follow-up conferences.

- Ongoing mentoring with a master teacher, which is typically arranged by the content area supervisor. New teachers should expect the mentor to meet with them at regularly scheduled meetings to (1) offer constructive critiques of their lesson plans and classroom practices; (2) share materials, strategies, knowledge, and experience; and (3) be a sympathetic listener and counselor.

- Professional development opportunities and, in some cases, funding.

- Materials, tools, and equipment necessary for you to deliver the course content.

- Pertinent information about students in your class (Individualized Education Plans [IEP] for special needs students, lists of students with health issues or chronic discipline problems, etc.).

- Pertinent information about the school (faculty manual listing duties and responsibilities; schedules; discipline code; curriculum guide; academic performance standards; calendar of events; procedures and forms for ordering materials and for making health, guidance, and special services referrals).

What Are Your Personal Expectations?

Now that you have had a chance to see some of the things that will be expected of you, take some time and reflect on what you expect from teaching and enter those expectations in your journal. Specifically, you want to consider what you expect from

- Your principal
- Your content area supervisor
- Your mentor
- Your colleagues
- The parents of your students
- Yourself

What Can New Teachers Do to Meet Expectations?

At the beginning this may all seem somewhat overwhelming; however, there are steps that you can actually take prior to entering the classroom and throughout the school year that will help reduce your burden, lessen your anxiety, and help you meet these expectations. First, it's important that you be cognizant of exactly what is expected; then, be proactive in meeting those expectations.

Before School Begins

- Meet with your supervisor and/or building administrator and get the following:
    - A printed list of their expectations for you. If one is not available, take notes at the meeting and send a copy to your supervisor or administrator via email as a follow-up to ensure that you have the same understanding.
    - Copies of the texts and lists of materials, tools, and equipment available that you can use to support your teaching throughout the year.
    - A planning book so that you can begin immediately to plan for the year.
    - A list of audiovisual aids and technology available to you and clarification of how you can access them. It's also a good idea to get the name of the person who is responsible for the care and upkeep of the equipment and the procedure for having equipment repaired.
    - A class roster with student addresses, phone numbers, and assigned guidance counselors.
    - A list of students with special needs in your class and their IEPs.
    - A copy of the discipline code and procedures, the name of the individual in charge of discipline, and where the disciplinarian can be located and accessed.
    - A map of the school.
    - A copy of the school calendar, noting holidays and special events.
    - A list of dates students will be absent from your classroom for such activities as student assemblies, state standardized testing, health exams, pep rallies, guidance scheduling, midterm and final exams, and scheduled class trips.
    - A curriculum guide for your grade or content area.
    - A copy of the local, state, and national standards. (Refer to Table 3.1 on page 54.)
    - A roster of school personnel and where they are located. If you are going to work in a school district that has a large population of students who speak English as their second language, be sure to ask who you should contact to have communications (letters, conferences, directions for students, etc.) translated.
    - Copies of pertinent forms (such as discipline, health, guidance, and Child Study Team referral forms, lesson-plan format, requisition forms for supplies, and additional texts).
    - The procedure and forms for reporting absences.

Note: All of this information should be readily available and easy to access.

- If access to your classroom is possible, set up your classroom with attractive bulletin boards, learning centers, seating arrangements, personal areas for students (cubbies), designated storage areas for books and materials, and so on.
- Develop your classroom academic and behavioral expectations and post them in a highly visible location (grades K–6) or have them printed, ready for distribution (grades 7–12) on the first day. (See Chapter 2, Models 7 and 8.)

- Develop a list of classroom management routines for turning in homework, going to the nurse, going to the lavatory, handing in late work, taking attendance, storing materials and equipment, and so on. (See Chapter 2, Models 5 and 6.)

- Prepare letters of introduction to parents and have them ready for mailing on or before the first day. (You can be sure the parents will be impressed.) (See Chapter 9, Figures 9.1 and 9.2 on pages 188–189.)

- Prepare a welcome letter to your students and post it prior to the opening of school. (See Model 1: Welcome Letter to Students.)

- Use your plan book to develop an academic game plan. Map out the units of instruction for the year. These can, of course, be modified during the year. This plan will help you see the "big picture," lend continuity to your teaching, and allow you to order materials, books, and equipment in advance. (See Chapter 3.)

- Set up your grade book.

- Develop your first unit of instruction and prepare the first two weeks of lesson plans, including assessments and scoring rubrics. (See Chapter 3.)

- List the supplies and materials you will need for your first unit so that you can submit your requisition form on or before the first day of school.

- Develop an agenda for your first day. (See the next section for suggestions.)

- Prepare student name tags and put names on student folders.

- Develop and organize a substitute teacher folder or binder. Being a substitute teacher is very difficult, particularly in the upper grades where many students have turned "getting over on the substitute" into a fine art. Although administrators know this, they still expect substitutes to come into your classroom and provide meaningful instruction and good classroom management in your absence. You can help your substitute meet this expectation by providing a three-ring binder or an accordion folder with all the information that would be needed throughout the day. (See Model 2: Checklist for Substitute Teacher Folder and Model 3: Substitute Teacher Classroom Evaluation Form.)

Throughout the School Year

- Ask your supervisor to set aside time each quarter to review with you your progress toward meeting the expectations set for you.

- Maintain a weekly journal where you can record your thoughts, reactions, successes, disappointments, and reflections on how you can improve your teaching practices; your interactions with students, parents, and colleagues; and so on.

- To stay current, join a local, state, or national professional organization and subscribe to its journal.

- Attend a professional development meeting or conference. Most major conferences are posted in the professional journals and on their websites.

- Use rubrics to facilitate returning student work promptly. (See Chapter 4, pages 79, 83–85, and 91.)

At the End of the School Year

- Revisit expectations set for you and by you for the past school year. Identify those you met and reflect on ways you can meet the goals you were unable to reach.

- Meet with your supervisor to discuss your reflections and to get suggestions for helping you meet next year's expectations.

- Reward yourself for a job well done.

- Begin to prepare for the next year.

 ## The First Day: Setting the Expectations

As the saying goes, you only have one chance to make a first impression. What you do on the first day will set the tone for the days that follow. For this reason, it is considered by many teachers as the most important day of the year. You want students to leave your class with the impression that you are a kind, interesting, organized, knowledgeable person who has a great deal to offer them. Most important, you want them to think of your class as an event that they won't want to miss. A carefully planned first day is the first step to ensure this reaction. To this end, we strongly recommend you enter your classroom on the first day with a huge smile and a written agenda. What follows are some of the things you may want to include on your first day.

- A formal greeting, welcoming students to your world.

- A short introduction of yourself. Make it fun and interesting. Don't talk about your degrees or your philosophy of education—boring!

- Take attendance and assign seats. Having the seating chart completed before class begins saves a lot of time and makes you look very organized.

Suggestions for Introductory Activities

An introductory activity is a good idea for the first day, particularly in classes where the students do not know each other. It gives students an opportunity to be recognized without the pressure of thinking of something interesting to say, which usually accompanies those dreaded requests by teachers for students to introduce themselves. A well-planned introductory activity will also help you begin the process of personalizing your students in a fun and interesting way.

These activities are intended to be introductory only; therefore, each should be time limited. It's a good idea to bring a stopwatch to help you manage the time.

Activity 1 Student-to-Student Introductions

In pairs, have the students conduct mini-interviews of each other for five minutes. At the end of that time, have each student stand up and formally introduce his or her partner using the information garnered from the interview. Prior to the interviews, instruct the students to find out a minimum of four interesting things about their partners.

Activity 2 Most and Least Activity

Separate the class into pairs and give each student a list of most and least favorites to fill in for their partners. The list might include such items as candy bar, movie, actor, video game, and car. After five minutes, move around the room and ask students to share what they found out about their partners. Using an overhead projector and a transparency, a whiteboard, or a chalkboard, record common class likes and dislikes.

Activity 3 Beat the Clock

Divide the class into teams of three or four and give each team the same crossword puzzle to solve. After ten minutes, have the teams share results. You may want to award a prize (candy bar, extra credit points, stickers, etc.) to the winning team.

Activity 4 Me in a Bag

Give each student a paper lunch bag, four squares of paper, and a magic marker. Then, ask the students to draw something on each one of the squares that tells something about themselves and their interests. Students can either switch bags and guess the interests of their partners or share the contents of their own bag with the class.

Activity 5 Who or What Am I? (grades K–4)

Cut out pictures (famous people, animals, things) and tape a different picture on the back of each student. Then, give the students the opportunity to ask three people in the room for a hint to the identity of the person or thing in the picture. End the activity by bringing each child to the front of the room to guess the identity of the picture on his or her back.

Activity 6 Scavenger Hunt (grades K–4)

Divide the class into teams and give the teams a list of things that can be found in the classroom. Without moving from their seats, they must use their eyes only to find each item. Give the teams five minutes to find and record the locations on their answer sheets. For nonreaders, the answer sheets should be two vertical rows, one with a picture of the item to be located and the other with the picture of the location. Students should be directed to draw a line between the item and its location.

- Have an introductory activity. This is a great way for you to begin to identify and personalize your students. (See Suggestions for Introductory Activities.)

- Collect pertinent student data (grades 4–12). Use three-inch by five-inch index cards. They're easy to store and easy to transport. Save time by having the information you want on the cards already listed on the board (e.g., name, address, phone number, email address, emergency contact person and number, guidance counselor, homeroom). Handing cards out at the door as the students walk in also saves time. (See Model 4: Student Information Card.) To get this information from nonwriters, send the data form to the parents for completion along with their introductory letter. When asking for student information, only ask for information that you need and never ask for personal information that might be embarrassing for some students (e.g., What does your father do for a living? Can your parents read and write? Do you have your own bedroom?).

- Present a slide show of pictures of key personnel in the school (such as principal, vice principal, nurse, librarian, crossing guards, reading specialist, cafeteria staff, and bus drivers).

- Take Polaroid or digital photos of students to be used to personalize cubbies or assignment charts.

- Review procedures, routines, and expectations. For grades K–6, these should be displayed on a large poster in a prominent place in the room. For grades 7–12, these should be printed and distributed.

- Distribute and review the syllabus for the first month (grades 9–12).

- Distribute a student interest survey. (See Chapter 4, Model 23.)

- Assign jobs (grades K–5). Have students on a rotating basis be responsible for collecting homework, monitoring the hall, passing out paper, and other tasks.

- Distribute texts and cover books.

- Give students their first assignment.

Meeting expectations is integral to every aspect of teaching. From this day forward, you will be about the business of meeting expectation—expectations set for you by your building administrators, your immediate supervisors, your students and their parents, and, most important, expectations of competency and exemplary teaching that you will hopefully set for yourself.

Advice from the Field

The following is advice for new teachers garnered from a survey of 150 seasoned teachers with a total of 3,855 years of teaching experience.

- The more planning and busywork you can do before school begins, the more time you will have during the day and throughout the year to spend on what matters most—teaching children and working toward becoming an exemplary teacher!

- When setting up your grade book and game plan, include holidays and days your students will not be in your class.

- To avoid being distracted by students who arrive after class has started on the first day, it's a good idea to make up in advance five packets of everything you are going to distribute that day.

- Use your preparation period wisely. Have units done well in advance of their delivery. Make modifications immediately to lessons taught so that they will be ready for the next teaching year.

- Stay clear of faculty room gossip. It will always come back to haunt you.

- Make friends with the administrative and custodial staff. They're wonderful allies.

- Use the first few months of department meetings to quietly listen and learn. Seasoned teachers are quickly turned off by inexperienced teachers telling them what they should do.

- Develop a class website that parents and students who miss class can access to stay aware of class assignments and activities.

- To keep parents informed, use the school computer system to send a newsletter via mass mailing or send personal email messages to parents to apprise them of student problems or successes. Ask your administrator or supervisor if approval is needed in advance for mass mailings. Be sure to keep hard copies of everything you send.

References

Allington, R. L., & Cunningham, P. M. (2002). *Schools that work: Where all children read and write* (2nd ed.). Boston: Allyn & Bacon.

Barnes, D., Britton, J., & Torbe, M. (1989). *Language, the learner, and the school.* Portsmouth, NH: Boynton/Cook.

Beach, R. (1993). *A teacher's introduction to reader-response theories.* Urbana, IL: National Council of Teachers of English.

Blanchowicz, C. L. Z. (1986). Making connections: Alternatives to vocabulary notebooks. *Journal of Reading, 29,* 643–649.

Clay, M. M. (1991). *Becoming literate: The construction of inner control.* Portsmouth, NH: Heinemann.

Clay, M. M. (1985). *The early detection of reading difficulties* (3rd ed.). Portsmouth, NH: Heinemann.

Fish, S. E. (1980). *Is there a text in this class?: The authority of interpretive communities.* Cambridge, MA: Harvard University Press.

Fisher, P. J. L., Blanchowicz, C. L. Z., & Smith, J. C. (1991). Vocabulary learning in literature discussion groups. In J. Zutell & S. McCormick (Eds.), *Learner factors/teaching factors: Issues in literacy research and instruction* (40th Yearbook of the National Reading Conference, pp. 201–209). Chicago: National Reading Conference.

Galda, L., Cullinan, B. E., & Strickland, D. S. (1993). *Language, literacy and the child.* Orlando, FL: Harcourt, Brace.

Gamoran, A. (1986). Instructional and institutional effect of ability grouping. *Sociology of Education, 59,* 185–198.

Gardner, H. (1983). *Frames of mind: The theory of multiple intelligences.* New York: Basic Books.

Goodlad, J. (1984). *A place called high school.* New York: McGraw-Hill.

Harkrader, M. A., & Moore, R. (1997). Literature preferences of fourth graders. *Reading Research and Instruction, 36*(4), 352–399.

Huck, C. S., & Kuhn, D. Y. (1968). *Children's literature in the elementary school.* New York: Holt, Rinehart and Winston.

Marzano, R. J., & Marzano, J. S. (1988). *A cluster approach to elementary vocabulary instruction.* Newark, DE: International Reading Association.

McCullough, M. A. (2002). Influences on how readers respond: An analysis of nationality, gender, text, teacher, and mode of response in four secondary school literature classrooms in the Netherlands and the United States. Unpublished doctoral dissertation, Rutgers University, New Brunswick, NJ.

Nagy, W., & Scott, J. (2001). Vocabulary processes. In M. L. Kamil, P. B. Mosenthal, P. D. Pearson, & R. Barr (Eds.), *Handbook of reading research* (Vol. 3, pp. 269–283). New York: Longman.

Piaget, J. (1995). *The essential Piaget.* H. G. & J. J. Voneche (Eds.). Northvale, NJ: Jason Aronson.

Rosenblatt, L. (1976). *Literature as exploration* (4th ed.). New York: Noble & Noble.

Skinner, B. F. (1974). *About behaviorism.* New York: Random House.

Strickland, D. S., Galda, L., & Cullinan, B. E. (2004). *Language arts: Learning and teaching.* Belmont, CA: Wadsworth/Thompson.

Vygotsky, L. S. (1986). *Thought and language.* Cambridge, MA: MIT Press.

Wheelock, A. (1992). *Crossing tracks: How untracking can save America's schools.* New York: New Press.

Welcome Letter to Students

Dear Sandra:

My name is Ms. Bartlett, and I am going to be your third-grade teacher this year. I have a lot of wonderful and exciting things planned for you and your classmates. We're going to be learning math, science, history, and geography. We're also going to be reading some fascinating books about children your age who live in other countries. You're even going to be given a personal pen pal so that you can write to a boy or girl in another country. I will share the other fun things we will be doing together when I meet you on September 15.

I am enclosing a special name tag for you to wear on the first day of school. I will be wearing the same name tag with my name on it so that you will be able to recognize me.

I'm looking forward to meeting you. Till then, have a good rest of the summer!

Sincerely,
Ms. Bartlett

Checklist for Substitute Teacher Folder

Include the following items in your substitute teacher folder:

_____ schedule and room assignments

_____ class roster and seating chart

_____ copy of homeroom and classroom procedures

_____ list of students in the class who require special attention and specific directions for accommodating those needs

_____ list of classroom monitors

_____ bus assignments and procedures

_____ lesson plans with clear and specific directions (Typically five days of plans are required, with all assignments photocopied in advance for the substitute.)

_____ map of the school and copy of the school calendar

_____ list of key personnel (principal, nurse, guidance staff, Child Study Team, disciplinarian, etc.) and where they can be located

_____ discipline report form

_____ hall passes

_____ list of emergency procedures

_____ substitute teacher evaluation form (See Model 3: Substitute Teacher Classroom Evaluation Form.)

Substitute Teacher Classroom Evaluation Form

Thank you for taking charge of my class for the day. It's important to me that my class runs smoothly in my absence. Therefore, I would appreciate your taking a few minutes to share with me your impressions of the day.

Thank you,
Ms. Bartlett

Name: _____ Date: _____

Class: _____

1. Did you find the Substitute Folder helpful?   Yes ___ No ___

2. Were the lesson plans complete and easy to follow?   Yes ___ No ___

3. Did you have the materials, texts, and equipment needed to teach the lesson?   Yes ___ No ___
   If not, what was missing? _____

4. Did any interruptions prevent the lesson from being completed?   Yes ___ No ___
   If so, please explain. _____
   _____

5. Were the students cooperative and well behaved?   Yes ___ No ___
   If not, please explain. _____
   _____

6. Please identify the students who were problematic. _____
   _____

7. Please identify the students who were particularly helpful. ___
   _____

8. What did you enjoy most about your day? _____
   _____

   Comments and suggestions for improvement: _____
   _____
   _____

Student Information Card

Information Card (Front)

Name _____ Homeroom _____

Student ID number _____

Address _____

Telephone number _____

Email address _____

Guidance counselor _____

Emergency contact person _____ Phone number _____

Information Card (Back)

Period	Room	Teacher	Subject	M	T	W	Th	F
1	B12	Johnson	English 1	X	X	X	X	X
2	C18	Jacks	Music		X		X	
3	GYM	Anderson	PE	X	X	X	X	X

Classroom Management

The Importance of Good Classroom Management

Classroom management is important for three very good reasons. One, a well-managed classroom means the difference between loving your job or leaving at the end of each day feeling defeated and depressed; two, a well-managed classroom maximizes your instructional time and sets the stage for you to be able to teach effectively; and three, a well-managed classroom speaks volumes when it comes to being asked to return the following year. No matter how brilliant you may be or how strong your credentials, if you can't manage your classroom, you probably

will not be asked back. Teachers and administrators may disagree about many things, but on the importance of classroom management, they are in total agreement. Professionals in the field come to understand very quickly that effective teaching and learning can only happen in a well-managed classroom.

What makes classroom management so important is that it encompasses so many facets of a teacher's day. At one time, the concept of classroom management referred to classroom decorum and discipline. This definition has been expanded over time to include how teachers organize and manage instruction; the physical layout of the classroom; daily classroom procedures and operations; instructional and noninstructional time; texts, equipment, and support materials; and, in some cases, paraprofessional assignments.

 ## *I*dentifying Your Management Needs

Becoming an effective classroom manager, like everything else, happens over time and requires planning that is both strategic and reflective. The most successful teachers have a clearly defined management plan in place, which they review and modify each year, prior to entering the classroom.

Because teachers are individuals with different tolerances, expectations, personalities, and ways of interacting with people, there is no one absolute management system that works for everybody. Therefore, as a new teacher, you need to develop a system for managing your classroom that works best for you. A good way to approach this is with a reflective self-assessment to identify the optimal conditions (both physical and behavioral) under which you anticipate you can teach with a high degree of effectiveness. Knowing in advance exactly what will make you successful will allow you to plan for success instead of just hoping that it happens. Begin your self-assessment by listing your needs:

- *Environmental needs* (e.g., a round table for conferencing, ample storage area, filing cabinets)
- *Instructional needs* (daily newspapers, computers, supplemental texts, state and national standards, etc.)
- *Student behavioral needs* (list of rules; for example, students need to [1] be on time, [2] follow directions, [3] be respectful, [4] complete homework assignments)
- *Personal needs* (e.g., a break every two hours, released time for doctor's appointments, a room with air conditioning)
- *Professional needs* (released time to attend graduate school, registration fees for professional conferences, ongoing mentoring, etc.)

Note: This assessment is specific to you and must support your personal comfort level. It stands to reason that if you are not comfortable in your environment, you will be less capable of managing it effectively. Once you have identified your needs, you can begin to explore possible ways to meet your needs before you actually begin teaching.

Managing Instructional Space

Classroom design depends largely on the physical size of the room as well as the size and the amount of furniture and equipment that you need to accommodate within that space. Regardless of how much or how little you have, you need to consider the following when organizing your classroom:

1. When organizing the student seating, make sure that you have an unobstructed view of *all* of the students at *all* times.

2. Arrange seating so that all of the students have a comfortable view of you. Students become distracted and frustrated when they have to constantly shift in their seats or crane their necks to see what is happening.

3. For safety, make sure that both you and the students can move freely between the desks or tables.

4. Make sure students can easily exit the room in an emergency. (The doorway should be clear at all times, and the window ledges should be able to be easily cleared.)

Note: Arranging desks and equipment is only a part of managing classroom space. The physical appearance of the room is equally important. It sends a message to everyone who enters the room about your feelings about the importance of the space and the things that go on within it. Plants, pictures, posters, and student artwork will make the room more interesting and inviting to everyone, including yourself.

Organizing Space for Instruction

For optimal learning, arrange student seating within the classroom to support your instructional activity.

- *Rows* are good for any activity that requires that you have the students' undivided attention (during direct instruction, modeling, testing, etc.). Because rows limit students' line of vision, they are not an optimal design for class discussions.

- A *large circle* provides a clear line of vision between students and is good for activities in which you want students to interact with each other (during performances, exhibitions, demonstrations, class discussions, or meetings).

- *Small groups* of three to four students provide for optimal participation because they afford everyone the opportunity and time to speak. For this reason, they are ideal for small-group discussions and projects.

Note: Changing the classroom design is a winning teaching strategy. It adds interest and stimulates participation, while it accommodates and supports the lesson objectives. However, like everything else in teaching, for this strategy to be effective, it needs to be planned. To save time and avoid confusion, have the room set up in the formation that supports your teaching for the day *prior* to the students' entering the room. If you want them to sit in designated seats, photocopy a seating chart and hand it out as the students enter the room. This way they can go directly to their seats so that you can begin class on time.

Organizing Space for K–5

In addition to considering how the desks will be organized for instruction, K–5 teachers who support their teaching with literacy centers must also consider how to organize these centers within the classroom (see Chapter 5). Typically, these centers are set up around the perimeter of the room. Because many teachers do not have a large enough room to accommodate multiple learning centers, they need to *create* space for students to work. Keep in mind that literacy centers are places where students go to practice the skills and concepts taught in class and that the centers change throughout the school year as the lessons and units change. You don't always need a lot of space to have productive literacy centers. The following suggestions may help you create literacy centers with very little space:

- Put a tablecloth for students to sit on, books, materials, and directions into a book bag for an instant literacy center.

- Attach metallic letters or numbers to the side of a metal filing cabinet for a literacy center where students can practice their math or word skills.

- Fill a large cookie tin or colorful gift bag with flashcards and provide large placemats or carpet squares for students to sit on, and you have a literacy center.

- Place a small blanket or carpet squares, tape recorders, headsets, and audiotapes next to an outlet to create a listening center.

- Empty a low cabinet and put in it the materials needed, directions, and a sectioned piece of colorful material for students to sit on, and you have a literacy center.

- Provide an overhead projector, transparencies, and oil pens to create a literacy center where students can collaborate to compose a story or make a puzzle or word game they can share with the class.

- Fill a plastic crate with interesting books and a blanket for students to sit on, and you have a literacy center.

- Cover a part of a wall or the back of a closet door with construction paper and give students words printed on cards backed with double-sided tape, and you have a literacy center where students can practice grammar and sentence construction.

Note: You don't need a lot of space to have meaningful literacy centers. You just need to look at the space that you have differently. Children are perfectly happy sitting on the floor, as long as they have something that they can sit on that defines their individual space (such as a carpet square, a placemat, a segment of a piece of material, a blanket, or a tablecloth that has been sectioned with a magic marker or masking tape, etc.).

 # Managing the Daily Operations of Your Classroom

Being well organized saves time, eliminates stress, and keeps students focused. In addition, a well-organized classroom makes students feel safe, comfortable, and secure. Knowing what to do and when and how to do it eliminates confusion and the possibility of error, which inevitably results in frustration and contention. Here are some helpful suggestions.

For Grades K–5

- Create and post a daily or weekly schedule of activities, and assign time frames to the activities to help students learn how to manage their own time.

- Assign monitors for classroom duties such as watering the plants, shutting down computers, collecting assignments, and distributing class work. (See Model 5: Duty Management System: Helping Hands.)

- Create guidelines and procedures for bathroom breaks, handing in class assignments and homework, moving between classes, participating in class discussions, and getting your attention when you are working with other students. (See Model 6: Classroom Procedures for K–5.)

- Identify for students where materials are to be stored and the procedure for putting things away.

- Hang a poster of behavior expectations in the front of the room and review it frequently. (See Model 7: Behavior Expectations for K–6.)
- Provide written instructions and review directions and performance expectations at the beginning of each assignment.
- Provide models for all student assignments so that they have a clear understanding of what they are expected to do.
- Provide activities for students to choose from during free time.
- Clarify for students how to get extra help.
- Print in-class and homework assignments on the board each morning before class and make reviewing the assignments a part of your daily routine.
- Provide an opportunity for students to have input into classroom organization, either with a suggestion or comment box or during a scheduled class meeting.

For Grades 6–12

- Provide students with a syllabus at the beginning of each unit, identifying goals, expectations, assignments, and due dates.
- Clarify for students how the class will be run. For example, you may want to begin each class with an objective quiz, which will be followed by student discussions in small response groups. If you change formats, alert the students the day before and provide them with detailed instructions. If the change requires a change in seating, provide a seating chart to save valuable class time the next day.
- Provide models and scoring rubrics with each assignment so that students will have a clear understanding of what they are expected to do before they begin the task.
- Provide students with a written explanation of the grading procedures.
- Provide students with a printed summary of their grades at the end of each quarter.
- Review policies regarding tardiness and absenteeism, class trips, and so on.
- Clarify behavior expectations. (See Model 8: Classroom Expectations for 6–12.)
- Clarify the guidelines for fire drills, lavatory breaks, makeup work, and so on.
- Identify a specific time and place you will be available for extra help. Provide a sign-up sheet with designated times so that students won't be wasting valuable time waiting for a conference.

- Provide an opportunity for students to express their opinions and make suggestions regarding classroom activities and procedures. This could be done by providing a suggestion or comment box, by holding an informal class meeting, or by having students comment in their journals.

Managing Time and Instruction

Managing time and instruction, two topics that are interrelated and integral to good classroom management, are discussed in context in Chapter 3, "Planning for Success."

Managing Paraprofessionals

A survey of chief school officers conducted in 1999 by the National Resource Center for Paraprofessionals indicated the existence of more than 500,000 full-time paraeducator positions in all content area programs in schools throughout the United States (Pickett, 1999). This number continues to increase significantly as schools turn to paraprofessionals to support academic teachers and their schools' federal mandate to leave no child behind. Although schools have employed teacher aides for over forty years, what has changed markedly is the services these men and women provide each day to support the classroom teacher. No longer limited to keeping records, preparing materials, maintaining equipment, or monitoring students in lunchrooms, hallways, or lavatories, teacher aides now are seen as paraprofessionals who participate in the learning process and in the delivery of direct services to learners and their parents (Moshoyannis, Pickett, & Granick, 1999). Today, paraprofessionals instruct learners in small and large groups, assist with assessment activities, administer standardized tests, and document learner performance (Moshoyannis et al., 1999; Pickett, 1999).

Should a paraprofessional be assigned to work with you, keep in mind that you are the primary teacher in the classroom. Paraprofessionals are there to assist and support teachers. They are not intended, nor are they qualified, to develop curriculum and instruction or to be the sole implementer of an instructional program. In addition, keep in mind that not all schools have prerequisites for paraeducators that include coursework in classroom management or in teaching and learning. It is important that you find out what the school policy is and what the academic preparation of your assistant is before making decisions about how you want the paraprofessional to support you and your teaching. If paraprofessionals in your

Suggestions for Managing Paraprofessionals

1. Meet with your paraprofessional prior to the opening of school to make decisions about how the paraprofessional's time will be spent. Prior to this meeting, list the roles, duties, and responsibilities you would like the paraprofessional to have in your classroom and ask that the paraprofessional bring a similar list to the meeting. This way, you will both have a clear vision of each other's expectations as well as talking points, which you can use to negotiate a common understanding.

2. Following the meeting, provide the paraprofessional with a written description, explicitly detailing the roles, duties, and responsibilities that you have agreed on. Copies of this description should also be given to your supervisor and building administrator to ensure that everyone has a common understanding.

3. Provide the paraprofessional with copies of your lesson plans in advance so that he or she can prepare. Share any difficulties you foresee students having and discuss the paraprofessional's role in resolving the problems.

4. Discuss with the paraprofessional your philosophy about classroom decorum and discipline and provide a copy of your behavior-management plan.

5. Meet at least once a week with your paraprofessional to ensure that you agree on your goals and expectations. It's important to designate a specific time each week for this meeting and to include it in your weekly agenda to ensure that the meeting does, indeed, take place.

6. Provide the paraprofessional with constructive evaluations of his or her work. Unless you have supervisory credentials and authorization from your school, these evaluations should be handled as informal discussions, identifying both strengths and weaknesses. It is important that if something needs to be remediated, you offer specific suggestions for doing so.

7. Provide training for your paraprofessional. For example, if you want that person to lead the class in a book walk, you need to provide instruction clarifying exactly how to do a book walk, or if you see a professional conference or a course that would be beneficial, ask your supervisor or administrator to arrange for your paraprofessional to attend.

8. Always treat your paraprofessional as a professional. Be sure to make requests, not dictate orders. Don't hesitate to solicit his or her opinions and suggestions. Although the person may not be degreed, many paraprofessionals have years of valuable experience in the classroom that you could use to enhance your teaching and classroom management skills.

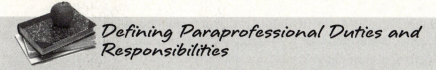

Defining Paraprofessional Duties and Responsibilities

When meeting with your paraprofessional to identify duties and responsibilities, you may want to consider the following:

Instructional Duties and Responsibilities	Noninstructional Duties and Responsibilities
Conduct book walks and read-alouds.	Manage record keeping (attendance, grades, hall passes, etc.).
Assist students with research and projects.	Manage equipment.
Help students edit their work.	Monitor students in the lavatory, hallways, and lunchrooms.
Respond to student questions.	Prepare materials (photocopy, collate, organize, etc.).
Document student learning using rubrics.	Set up literacy centers.
Tutor students individually and in small groups.	Attend to students who have special needs.
Research and provide background information on given topics.	Attend to students who are disruptive.
Listen to and monitor children as they practice skills.	Manage classroom organization and clean-up.
Ask probing questions that will assist student understanding of texts.	Organize and attend class functions and trips.
Assist with the administration of tests.	Order materials requested by the teacher.
Help students select activities once they have completed their work.	Escort students to the office, library, gym, pull-out classrooms.
Monitor and support student work in literacy centers.	Prepare bulletin boards and student work displays.
Participate in parent-teacher conferences.	Monitor and manage students' makeup work.
Participate in Child Study Team meetings.	Help monitor students during schoolwide drills.

school district have a negotiated contract that outlines the parameters of their work assignments, be sure to review the parameters before you ask a paraprofessional to do something that would be in violation of the contract.

Note: As you are working with your paraprofessional to define and establish the expectations and boundaries of your relationship, keep in mind that the ultimate goal is to create a positive work environment for you, your paraprofessional, and the students you both serve. This can best be accomplished through clearly defined roles, mutual respect, and a strong commitment to the educational process.

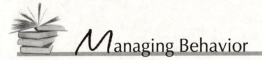

Managing Behavior

Identifying Your Management Style

Before you begin to develop your personal classroom management plan, you need to consider some important issues. One very important issue is how you plan to interact with your class. Inexperienced teachers often make the mistake of using strategies that intimidate and control student behavior. They clearly do not understand the monumental difference between controlling a class and managing a class. Nor do they understand the ramifications of opting for control. Control is used to obtain compliance and blind obedience and is easily accomplished with the use of threats and intimidation, which most often are executed with the basic *if–then* declarative statement. Sometimes these threats invoke the wrath of a higher authority: "If you don't sit down, I'm going to send you to the office" or "If you don't stop talking, I'm going to call your parents." Sometimes these threats involve the possibility of punishment: "If you get out of your seat one more time, you're not going on the field trip tomorrow" or "If I have to speak to you again, I'm deducting points from your grade." Sometimes these threats are veiled in questions that give the illusion that the student has a choice: "Remember what happened the last time you didn't finish your work?" or "Do I have to give you more work to keep you quiet?" Regardless of how these threats are presented, they are the least effective way to manage a classroom. Threats always set up an adversarial relationship between the student and the teacher, one in which the teacher may appear to win; however, the win is a hollow victory. You may get the child to comply, but the child, being human, will respond to the threat by being upset or angry. In either case, your student will not be in the frame of mind necessary to learn, which is, after all, your primary objective as a teacher.

A more effective way to manage your class is with challenging lessons that are interesting, active, and student-centered. Children who are actively engaged in their own learning are less likely to create problems. You will find that problems erupt quickly when children are bored or frustrated. Equally important, students need to feel successful. No one wants to feel like a failure, no matter what the age. If you see that a student is having difficulty, address the issue immediately *before* it becomes a failure. Having ongoing assessments will quickly alert you to problems in student learning so that you can give the student extra help and avoid unnecessary failure. (See Chapter 4 for suggestions.) This will also validate for your students that you care about them and about their learning, something all students, whether they will admit it or not, want from their teachers. The bottom line is success feels good, and children who feel good about themselves will want to come to your class every day and they'll want to please you and themselves by completing their work and by being a valued member of the class.

Developing a Behavior Management Plan

Like knowing what will make you successful, knowing what will impede your success is equally important. A vital step in this developmental process, then, should be to identify possible student behaviors that you think will be deterrents to your success. Once you have identified potential problems, begin to organize your personal management plan in three parts. Under Part 1, identify those conditions that would interfere with your ability to be an effective teacher. No condition should be considered too trivial to make this list. Teachers often find that it's the little things that are most irritating and distracting to their teaching. Under Part 2, identify what measures you could take to prevent the interference. You will find that many problems can be avoided or at least minimized by simply putting in place preventive measures at the onset of the class. Finally, under Part 3, identify what action you would take should the preventive measure not work. See Table 2.1 for a sample behavior management plan.

It's important to remember that a behavior management plan is a work in progress. You will need to revisit and reevaluate your plan frequently to identify procedures that worked well for you and to modify those that did not. Understand that it will take several years to shape your plan into a reliable document that you can refer to with confidence.

Teaching Good Behavior

At the beginning of the school year, in addition to giving students classroom procedures and guidelines, it's a good idea to give them actual training in good classroom conduct. You can't always assume that children understand what good classroom conduct is. Nor can you assume that they have a repertoire of behavioral alternatives. Having student-centered lessons dedicated to behavior gives

Table 2.1 Behavior Management Plan

Undesirable Conditions	Preventive Measure	Corrective Measure
Students running around room	1. Give students expectation of walking on the first day and clarify the danger to students and others. 2. Verbally reinforce behavior expectations daily at the beginning of class until learned.	*First offense:* Correct verbally with explanation. *Second offense:* Time out. *Third offense:* Behavior conference with student, self-assessment, and monitoring.
Students interrupting (calling out inappropriately)	1. Give students expectation of not interrupting on the first day. 2. Verbally reinforce behavior expectations daily at the beginning of class until learned. 3. Model behavior.	*First offense:* When student calls out, reiterate the rule with explanation and call on someone else for the response. *Second offense:* Behavior conference. *Third offense:* Time out and call parent.
Students bullying other students (verbally, nonverbally, physically)	1. Show film on bullying on second day of class and discuss the seriousness of bullying. 2. Model respectful behavior.	*First offense:* Detention, behavior conference, and call home. *Second offense:* Send to principal's office.
Students not staying on task	1. Check that the assignment is not too difficult and that students have the skills in place to be successful. 2. Make sure directions are complete and understandable. 3. Check student records to identify students who may have problems in this area and monitor them as they are doing the assignment to help them stay on task.	*First offense:* Conference with student to determine the source of the problem. *Second offense:* Behavior conference, student self-assessment, and monitoring. *Third offense:* Contact guidance counselor for suggestions and support.

Undesirable Conditions	Preventive Measure	Corrective Measure
Students coming to class unprepared	1. Discuss the importance of coming to class prepared on the first day. 2. Require students to keep a home-work to-do list in the front of their notebooks. 3. Inform parents that students will be receiving nightly assignments and ask for their assistance in checking that they are done. 4. Come to class prepared every day.	*First offense:* Conference with student to see if there is a problem. *Second offense:* Contact parent or guidance counselor for suggestions and support. *Third offense:* Detention.
Students not paying attention	1. Do not begin speaking until everyone is paying attention. 2. Stand by students who tend to not pay attention. 3. Check student records to identify students who have had this problem in the past and make sure you have their attention before beginning.	*First offense:* Conference with student. Give student personal cue that could be used to redirect attention. *Second offense:* Contact guidance counselor for suggestions and support to help student focus. *Third offense:* Notify parents of the problem.
Students destroying property	1. Clarify expectation for respect of property on the first day. 2. Model respect for student property.	*First offense:* Send to principal's office and notify parents.
Students coming to class late	1. Discuss expectation on the first day. 2. Always be on time and start class on time every day.	*First offense:* Verbal warning. *Second offense:* Behavior conference. *Third offense:* Detention, contact guidance office and parents.
Students refusing to participate	1. Ensure students understand the rationale and benefits of the assign-ment and for participating. 2. Sit students next to students who will participate. 3. Give students a specific task or job.	*First offense:* Conference to determine why the student does not want to participate. Provide student with strategies for participation. *Second offense:* Joint conference with guidance counselor. *Third offense:* Parent conference.
Students who do not work cooperatively in groups	1. Assign everyone in the group a specific task.	*First offense:* Conference and mentor student and provide cooperative learning strategies.

students an opportunity to think about behavior and learn new ways of conducting themselves while at school. Your lessons could include the following:

1. Lead a class discussion about behavior, beginning each segment of the discussion with "What should a student do if . . . ?"

2. Give students scenarios and ask them in small groups to discuss how the student behaving badly could solve his or her problem in a more productive way.

3. Give groups of students scenarios and ask them to write and act out two skits, one showing a negative behavior and the other, an alternative way to behave.

4. Give students a list of problems. Next to each problem, provide a negative strategy for dealing with the problem and ask them to think of a more appropriate alternative behavior.

5. Invite a guest speaker or a panel of speakers who are authorities on behavior (school psychologist, social worker, local psychiatrist) to come into your high school class to discuss behavior and why people behave the way they do.

Correcting Behavior Problems

Very often, you can resolve a minor problem such as inappropriate talking by merely moving toward and standing next to the offender, or standing quietly waiting for the class's attention, or using cues such as raising the volume of your voice or holding your hand above your head. Sometimes, a simple "May I please have your attention?" is enough to bring the class to order without resorting to a disciplinary action. Intuitive students will actually observe you modeling good behavior and follow suit. Other times, however, you will have to take more direct action. Before you do, make sure that the corrective measure is appropriate for the offense. Talking in class, for example, merits a less extreme corrective measure than does verbally attacking another student. Take time to consider what will be minor and major offenses in your class and what corrective measures you are going to attach to each offense. The following are some options to consider for minor offenses.

- *Assign Time Outs.* Having a private area in the classroom where children can be sent to "cool off" is particularly effective for students who have been managed with time outs at home. Students should be required to be reflective during time out. A condition of leaving time out should be either a verbal or written acknowledgment of the offense and possible alternative ways the student could have handled the situation.

- *Enter into a Behavioral Contract with the Student.* This strategy, which requires that the teacher and student meet and negotiate behavior, is an effective way to have students take responsibility for their own actions. The teacher and student agree on the desired behavioral outcomes and time lines as well as the rewards and penalties for meeting or failing to meet the contractual obligations.

- *Change Classroom Seating.* Sometimes, just rearranging the seats in the classroom, separating students who negatively influence each other, is an easy resolution to discipline problems.

- *Have Offenders Self-Monitor.* This strategy engages students in monitoring and correcting their own behavior. The teacher meets with the student regularly to review and discuss the student's self-monitoring record and to explore alternative ways of managing the problems that led to the offender's undesirable behavior. (See Model 9: Student Self-Monitoring Record.)

- *Send the Students to Their Guidance Counselors for Behavioral Counseling.* This is an appropriate strategy for students who need more time and more in-depth counseling than you are able to give.

- *Hold Class Meetings.* This is a wonderful way to have the members of the class participate in managing classroom decorum and discipline. Giving students the opportunity to engage in an open dialogue regarding appropriate behavior and penalties empowers them by giving a sense of control and a vested interest in conforming to the guidelines they helped develop.

- *Acknowledge Good Behavior.* Everyone enjoys recognition and praise. Acknowledging students individually for their good behavior is possibly one of the simplest and most effective ways of managing classroom discipline.

There may be times, however, when these remedial strategies do not work. When that happens, you need to resort to more punitive measures. *Note:* Punishment is only in order when you have exhausted *all* other options.

Punitive Measures

- Take away school privileges such as going on a class trip or participating in sports or after-school activities. Participating in activities is not, as some students think, a right; it is a privilege that must be earned with good grades and good behavior.

- Assign detention after school.

- Send students to in-school detention or suspension.
- Have the student removed from the classroom until a joint conference is held with the parents, student, and school administrator.
- Send the student to the principal's office. Although necessary at times, it should be your last option.

There are three important things to remember about punishment. (1) The goal of punishment should be to correct behavior. Whatever the punishment, it should be temporary: students should know that they have the opportunity to regain their privileges with remediated behavior. (2) Academic work should NEVER be used as punishment. Punishing students by having them read an extra book or by writing an essay, for example, sends the wrong message. We want students to see academics as fun and rewarding, not punitive. (3) Whatever choices you make regarding punishment, make sure they are consistent, fair, and within the framework of your school's policy.

Handling Severe Discipline Problems

In a perfect world, there would be no severe behavior problems, but unfortunately, that's not the world teachers live in. At one time or another, every teacher, regardless of experience, encounters discipline problems that cannot be handled with mediation. It is important to be prepared. Read the discipline code and procedures *before* you enter the classroom for the first time. Find out who is in charge of discipline in your school and how you contact that person should the need arise. Don't wait until you have a volatile situation in your class to find out what you should do or who you should contact. For your safety and the safety of your students, you need to have an action plan in place for major infractions. Discuss this plan with your supervisor and the person who is in charge of discipline to ensure you are all in agreement.

Dealing with Students Who Are Out of Control

There may be times when you might encounter a student who is either belligerent or out of control. When this happens, an immediate response is necessary. Most important, you need to remain calm. A screaming teacher exacerbates the situation and gives the other students the impression that the teacher is also out of control. What you want to do first is try to isolate the student who is causing the disturbance in a nonconfrontational way. This can usually be accomplished by asking the student to step outside the door, which will give you the opportunity to get the student calmed down so that you can find out what happened and begin working on a resolution to the problem. If the child refuses to comply, you will need to call the office for assistance. Even if the problem is resolved, it is important that you follow up on the incident. Approach the student, either later in the day or the next day, to discuss what happened and to explore alternate strategies that the student could have used to resolve the problem that led to the disturbance. Sometimes students act out because they need help and they don't know how to ask for it. An unfortunate reality is that you will probably have students at one time or another who are living in abusive or destructive environments over which they have no control. In these cases, acting out is often a cry for help. If the student continues to present problems, you need to find out why. The guidance office and the principal's office are two good places to start to see if a history of discipline problems exists. You should also consult the Child Study Team and the school nurse to see if a medical problem or learning disability may be causing the child to act out. Talking with other teachers who have had the student will also give you valuable insights and possible strategies for handling future problems. You could also ask your department supervisor for advice. Once you have an understanding of the student's background, you need to contact the parents and ask them to come in for a conference, which should be attended by all the interested parties. For example, depending on the problem, the interested parties could include the student's guidance counselor, the discipline officer, the nurse, or the school psychologist. The student should also be invited to participate in this meeting. The important thing to remember is that you are not expected to resolve severe discipline problems on your own. You are, however, expected to be proactive and ask for help when you need it.

Rewarding Good Performance and Behavior

Too often, teachers are so busy with the demands of the job that they limit their teaching to correcting poor student behavior and performance. While it is important to make corrections, it is equally important to remember to let students know when they are doing something right. These rewards can come in different shapes and forms. Simple forms of acknowledgment such as applause, smiles, and high fives are easy to distribute and fun to give and to receive. Here are some other suggestions for showing your appreciation and approval.

For Grades K–6

1. Give students tokens and invite them to deposit one in a container at the front of the class each time they do or say something that deserves recognition. When the container is full, treat the class to a popcorn or an ice-cream party.

2. Send Performance Certificates home once a week to applaud good work or behavior.

3. Don't limit your phone calls to parents to those dealing with problems. Call them with good news and let them share in the joy of their child's success.

4. Give out Student of the Week awards and make sure everyone makes the list.

5. Reward the class with a class trip. Trips don't always have to be someplace special. A picnic on the school grounds can be just as much fun.

6. Give the class a homework-free pass for the weekend.

7. Place decorative stickers and stamps on work, which is always welcome.

For Grades 7–12

1. Make a special effort to see the student outside of class to compliment his or her work or behavior.

2. Send a special progress report home or call parents directly to share good news.

3. Reward the class with a special trip, guest speaker, or pizza party at the end of the quarter.

4. Ask students' permission to use their work as models for other students.

5. Make a point of having a conversation with your students about something other than class work. Find out what your students' interests are and make a point of showing your interest in them.

6. Reward the class for good work during the week with a homework-free weekend.

7. When talking to students about their work, remember to include compliments as well as criticisms. Whenever possible, try to express criticisms in the form of corrective suggestions. If you identify weaknesses in red ink, try highlighting strengths in blue or green so that students can see and take pride in the positives in their work.

Managing English Language Learners

1. Be sensitive to the possibility of cross-cultural miscommunications. Students may be responding to what they think you want them to do, which may not be the same as what you intend for them to do. An easy way to address this issue is by simply asking them to explain what they think the assignment is before

they begin. It's always a good idea to be prepared to give students directions in a variety of ways (verbal and visual) until you see that they understand.

2. Understand that communicating in a different language is tiring. After a period of time, your students may lose focus, not out of disinterest but out of exhaustion. These students may need more frequent breaks or some quiet downtime to regroup.

3. Engage your students in meaningful activities. Like all students, busy students are less likely to present problems. Have a host of planned activities at your fingertips that will promote their English language development.

4. Make sure that your language, tone, facial expressions, and gestures match the message you are communicating. Students with limited language proficiency depend on nonverbal cues to understand. They may misinterpret *loud* for *reprimanding* or a *rushed* expression for *annoyance* and become upset and then shut down.

5. Be aware that not understanding can lead to frustration, which can, in turn, cause English language learners to act out or shut down. When you see students becoming frustrated, approach them immediately and try to help them overcome whatever it is that is causing them difficulties.

Advice from the Field

- Always enter your classroom with a smile. Everyone responds favorably to a smile and a warm welcome. Your students are no exception.

- Introduce classroom and behavior management practices the first day of class and reinforce daily for at least the first two weeks of classes to ensure students have a clear understanding of how they will be operating for the remainder of the year.

- Always treat your students with respect. Always say "please" and "thank you" and expect your students to do the same. A good rule of thumb is to treat your students as you would like your own children to be treated.

- Always be clear. Say what you mean and mean what you say. If you want your students to sit down, do not ask them, "Do you want to take a seat?" With this question, you're inviting a response that most likely will be "no," rather than what you really want.

- Always be consistent. Students feel comfortable when they know what to expect.

- Always take an interest in your students. Make your students feel they are important. Ask about their activities outside the classroom. Notice when they're absent. Give them compliments.

- Always begin the term by assigning seats. One, this creates a degree of comfort for children by eliminating the "sit by me" syndrome that for popular students is a natural part of their day, but for the unpopular students never is; and, two, it helps you learn names quickly and expedites taking attendance.

- Always begin your class on time and insist that students arrive on time. This sends an immediate message to your students that what is going to be happening that day is important, and there's no time to be wasted.

- Always have something planned that contributes meaningfully to student learning. You can be sure that a free period or a movie that is unrelated to what is being learned will be interpreted as you not having anything planned. If you expect your students to come to class prepared, you must set the example by doing the same.

- Always make your expectations, both academic and behavioral, clear on the first day of class.

- Always explain the rationale for each expectation. If you don't have a better reason than "because I say so," it's a good idea to drop the expectation. Students, regardless of age, who understand why they are being asked to do something are more likely to comply if they see the wisdom in the request.

- Always be supportive. If you tell children they *can*, they *will*. Keep raising the bar and challenge your students to reach it. If students respect you, they will rise to the level of your expectations.

- Always applaud good work and good behavior.

- Don't scream. It's ineffective and it makes you look ugly.

- Don't ever put your hands on your students. Throwing objects at or near students is also a big no-no.

- Don't invade your students' space unless invited. Keep a professional distance. Unless there is a problem, stay out of their personal business.

- Don't be rude or sarcastic. Remember, you're the role model and students are quick to mimic what they see.

- Don't humiliate students. Don't post or read grades out loud. Don't call on students who you know don't know the answer. Don't make snide comments when they are wrong.

- Don't allow your students to harass other students. Never tolerate rude comments, snickers, laughs, or inappropriate eye rolling when another student is participating.

- Don't put yourself on a pedestal. If you make a mistake, admit it and move on.

- Don't be inflexible. There's often more than one way to do something. Applaud students who think out of the box instead of doing things exclusively "your way."

- Don't negotiate discipline. Make consequences clear on the first day and then stick to them.

- Don't allow yourself to say "If you do this one more time . . ." because that tells the student that he or she can commit the offense one more time.

- Don't try to be like your students. If you want to be respected, you have to command respect. Dress, act, and speak like an adult if you want to be treated like one. Remember: You can be with them but not of them.

- Don't be alone with students in your classroom without being clearly visible from a door, which should *always* be open. This invites misunderstandings that can lead to problems in and outside the classroom. Students, regardless of age, are impressionable and can easily misread your interest in them. The open door sends a clear message that your meeting is strictly professional. If you are going to be working with students after school, it's best to let someone in the office know.

- Don't be afraid to show that you have a sense of humor. Teaching is fun. Don't be afraid to show your students that you enjoy being with them and that teaching and learning gives you great pleasure.

Remember that your students have the same feelings you do, and they, like you, have good days and bad days. Respect their feelings. Give them space when they need it and support when they ask for it. Make your classroom a safe, comfortable, inviting place to be. If you think of your students as your guests and your classroom as a party where you're serving a plethora of academic goodies, you will find your classroom a pleasure and a place that you can easily manage.

Additional Resources

Bianco, A. (2002). *One-minute discipline: Classroom management strategies that work.* San
　　Francisco: Jossey-Bass, Inc.

Cangelosi, J. S. (2000). *Classroom management strategies.* New York: Wiley.

Emmer, E. T., Evertson, C. M., & Worsham, M. E. (2000). *Classroom management for second-*
　　ary teachers. Boston: Allyn & Bacon.

Evertson, C. M., Emmer, E. T., & Worsham, M. E. (2000). *Classroom management for*
　　elementary teachers. Boston: Allyn & Bacon.

Mackenzie, R. J. (2003). *Setting limits in the classroom: How to move beyond the dance of*
　　discipline in today's classroom. New York: Random House.

Payne, Ruby K. (2003). *A framework for understanding poverty.* Highlands, TX: Aha!
　　Process Inc.

Online Resources

Answers.com—www.answers.com/topic/classroom-management
4 Faculty—www.4faculty.org
Pro Teacher—www.proteacher.com
Electronic Learning Community—www.pgcps.org/~elec/gameplan.htm

References

Moshoyannis, T., Pickett, A. L., & Granick, L. (1999). *The evolving roles of education/training*
　　needs of teacher and paraprofessional teams in New York City Public Schools. New York:
　　Paraprofessional Academy, Center for Advanced Study in Education, Graduate Center,
　　City University of New York.

Pickett, A. L. (1999). *Strengthening and supporting teacher and paraeducator teams: Guidelines*
　　for paraeducator roles, supervision, and preparation. New York National Resource Center
　　for Paraprofessionals in Education and Related Services, Center for Advanced Study in
　　Education, Graduate Center, City University of New York.

Duty Management System: Helping Hands

Assignment	Responsibilities	Helpers
Teacher's Assistants	Pass out and collect papers, books, and materials.	Alan, Paula
Line Leader	Leads the line when students pass between classes.	Fred
Line Ender	Ends the line and ensures no one gets lost.	Alison
Door Holder	Holds door when class is coming and going.	Phileppe
Lavatory Monitor	Monitors behavior in boy's room and reports problems to teacher.	Richard
Lavatory Monitor	Monitors behavior in girl's room and reports problems to teacher.	Morgan
Refuse Collector	Passes trash can through the room at the end of the day.	Andrea
Librarian	Checks books in and out of class library during free time.	Ling
Horticulturalist	Waters the plants on Monday morning.	Roberto
Board Cleaner	Erases the blackboard at the end of the day.	William
Ichthyologist	Feeds the fish every morning.	Cassandra
Errand Runner	Runs errands for teacher.	Adam
Desk Monitor	Checks desks at the end of the day to ensure they are in place and have no writing on them.	Ryan
Time Keeper	Alerts teacher when it is time to clean up for the day.	Jared
Bulletin Board Attendant	Posts student work on the bulletin board.	Jeanette
Equipment Manager	Passes out and collects equipment during recess.	Peter
Substitute (1)	Substitutes for helper who is out.	Ken
Substitute (2)	Substitutes for helper who is out.	Maria

Classroom Procedures for K–5

What Do I Do If . . .

I want to ask a question?	**Raise your hand and wait patiently to be called on.**
I want to go to the lavatory?	**Sign your name in the lavatory book, take a pass, and walk quietly to the lavatory.**
I want to go to the nurse?	**Raise you hand and ask for a pass to the nurse.**
I want extra help?	**In class: Raise your hand and ask for help. After class: Extra help is available every Monday from 3:00 to 4:30. Just come in.**
I want a book to read?	**During Free Time, you can check a book out with our class librarian.**
I want to hand in my homework?	**Put your homework in the homework box as soon as you come into the class.**
I want a drink of water?	**Unless it is an emergency, please wait until break time.**

Behavior Expectations for K-6

Good Classroom Behavior

1. Always be polite. Say "please," "thank you," and "excuse me."

2. Always be respectful of other people's feelings. No mimicking, name-calling, making funny faces, or laughing at other classmates.

3. Always wait your turn. Raise your hand and wait quietly to be called on. Your turn will come.

4. Keep your hands to yourself. No touching, pushing, shoving, or hitting other students.

5. Always use your soft voice in the classroom.

6. Be where you are supposed to be when you are supposed to be there. No wandering around or getting lost.

7. No temper tantrums. If you are having a problem, talk to me and we will work together to solve the problem.

8. Stay in line with hands to your sides when we are moving between classes.

9. Always be safe. No throwing anything in the classroom.

10. Never bring anything dangerous to school like a knife, a gun, or an object with sharp edges.

Classroom Expectations for 6-12

I expect that all of my students will

- Come to class eager to read, ask questions, challenge, and debate the material presented.
- Challenge the limits of their own thinking.
- Be responsible for their own learning.
- Be open to other students' beliefs and opinions.
- Treat every member of our classroom community with sensitivity and respect.
- Work cooperatively in Reader Response groups.
- Work to develop strong literacy skills (analytical reading, writing, speaking, viewing, etc.)
- Be seated and ready to begin when the second bell rings.
- Come to class prepared *every day* with books, pens, notebooks, and journals.
- Complete and submit all assignments *on time*.
- Come in for extra help *immediately* when a problem arises.

Students can expect that I will

- Come to class every day prepared with a meaningful lesson.
- Provide instruction that supports local, state, and national standards.
- Begin and end class on time.
- Be open to conflicting arguments and opinions.
- Be fair and nonjudgmental.
- Provide a minimum of one week's notice prior to an exam.
- Return all written work within one week of receiving it.
- Provide scoring rubrics for all written assignments, projects, presentations, and so on, at the time the assignment is given.
- Be available for extra help in my classroom every Wednesday from 3:00 to 5:00.
- Provide students with grade sheets at the end of each quarter.
- Treat my students with respect.

Student Self-Monitoring Record

Name: _____

Behavior needing correction: _____

Date	What happened?	What caused it to happen?	How did you handle the problem?	How might you handle a similar problem in the future?

3

Planning for Success: Unit and Lesson Planning and Design

Why Plan?

Exemplary teaching doesn't happen by accident; it happens as a direct result of careful, thoughtful planning that is informed by content area expertise, a wide range of pedagogically sound strategies, and a clear understanding of how students

learn best. Although there are many reasons why teachers spend so much of their time planning, the most compelling reason is time. Once you begin the planning process, you will see very quickly how little instructional time you actually have in relation to the volume and scope of material you are expected to teach your students. When one thinks of 180 to 200 days, it may sound like a lot of time, but when you factor in holidays (Spring recess, Christmas recess, Thanksgiving, Rosh Hashanah, Yom Kippur, Martin Luther King Day, Memorial Day, Presidents' Day, etc.), educators' professional conference days, state testing days, parent-teacher conference days, days lost to inclement weather, half days for Back-to-School nights, and midterm and final exam weeks, your actual teaching time is greatly reduced. Add to that, time lost for class meetings, health screenings, assemblies, guidance appointments, fire drills, and scheduling for the following year and you will undoubtedly see the urgency in planning. Teachers who do not put the time and necessary effort into effective planning inevitably find themselves at the end of the year with a monumental list of things they "didn't get a chance to cover."

Another equally important reason for planning is that it allows teachers to visualize the content of their courses to ensure that all of the skills and concepts required by local, state, and national standards have been taught and that the individual learning styles and capabilities of all of their students have been given consideration in each unit of instruction. In addition, being able to visualize their teaching agenda helps teachers quickly see gaps in instruction, which impede the natural flow and continuity of the course. Ordering and scheduling are also made much easier with long-range lesson plans. Teachers who wait until the last minute to order materials or to schedule guest speakers and field trips often find that their needs cannot be accommodated.

Teachers also find that written lesson and unit plans, in addition to providing documentation accounting for curriculum and instructional practices, provide strategic talking points for one-on-one conferences, with mentors or supervisors, that are personal and class-specific. Teachers and supervisors tend to agree that conferences based on actual practices and curricular choices are much more satisfying and more productive than conferences based on generic comments or observations.

A final reason for teachers to plan effectively is a more personal one. Having instructional plans is like taking a trip with a clearly defined road map and itinerary, particularly for new teachers. Like any new adventure, you will find that traveling with a good map and a well-thought-out itinerary will provide you with a sense of comfort and security by reassuring you where you're going, when you're going, how you're going, and ultimately why you're making the trip.

Where Do I Begin?

The process of instructional planning should begin the moment you are given your teaching assignment. Once you know what you will be teaching, you need to immediately begin collecting all of the relevant information, sources, and materials that you will need to begin putting your program together. This list should include the following:

- A three-ring binder and a box of three-ring plastic binder sleeves for lesson plans and support materials. A binder is a great way to keep all your lesson plans, assessments, handouts, and support materials together. Having a separate binder for each unit makes it easy to access, store, review, and organize information for the following year.

- A ten-month working calendar for the school year.

- A copy of the school calendar for the year.

- Copies of all the textbooks you will be using throughout the year.

- Lists of the supplies and equipment available for your use.

- A list of the audiovisual materials available for your use.

- A list of the computer programs available for your use.

- A list of the current library materials available, which will be helpful when planning research and library assignments.

- A list of external sources (such as guest speakers, possible field trips, movies, documents) that you would like to incorporate into your program.

- A copy of the school's curriculum guide. *Note:* If the school does not have a written guide, use the state and national standards to guide your curricular choices.

- A list of the state and national standards. If your school does not have copies of the standards available for you, you can access them online at the following sites:
  - *Individual state standards:* www.statestandards.com
  - *National standards:* See Table 3.1 for a list of websites.

Now that you have everything you need, you are ready to begin the fun part—the actual planning process!

Table 3.1 National Teaching Standards

Discipline	Developers of Standards	Website
Art (visual and performance)	The American Alliance for Theater and Education, National Art Education Association, and the Music Educators National Conference	www.artsedge.kennedy-center.org/teach/standards
Economics	The National Council on Economic Education	www.ncee.org
English/Language Arts/Reading	The National Council of Teachers of English, the International Reading Association, and the University of Illinois Center for the Study of Reading	www.ncte.org
Foreign Languages	The American Council on the Teaching of Foreign Languages	www.actfl.org/14a/pages/index.cfm?pageid=3324
Geography	The Association of American Geographers, the National Council for Geographic Education, and the National Geographic Association	www.nationalgeographic.com/education/standards.html
Health	The Committee for National School Health Education Standards	www.aahperd.org/aahe/pdf_files/standards.pdf
History/Civics/Social Studies	The Center for Civic Education and the National Center for History in the Schools	www.sscnet.ucla.edu/nchs/standards
Mathematics	The National Council of Teachers of Mathematics	www.nctm.org/standards
Physical Education	The National Association of Sports and Physical Education	www.aahperd.org/naspe
Psychology	The American Psychological Association	www.cnets.iste.org/teachers/+_stands.html
Science	American Association for the Advancement of Science, the National Science Teachers Association, and the National Research Council's National Committee	www.nsta.org/standards
Technology	International Technology Education Association	www.apa.org/ed/topss/homepage.html

Step 1. Date your working calendar for the entire school year.

Step 2. On your working calendar, identify all the full or partial days that you will *not* be teaching (such as holidays, parent-teacher conference days, educator's conference days, professional development days, exam days). Be sure to identify days that have activities scheduled that will take students out of your classroom (such as pep rallies, assemblies, class scheduling, health screening days).

Step 3. Identify the units that you will be teaching. Schools typically identify in the curriculum guides the units you are expected to teach as well as the specific skills and concepts and the estimated time each unit should take. If your school does not have a curriculum guide, you will need to go to the state and national standards to identify the skills and concepts and organize them into logical, coherent units of study.

Step 4. Plot the units on your working calendar. There is no rule governing the length of a unit. Units can vary from being a week long to a month long or even longer, depending on the content and skills that need to be taught. These dates are best guesses. You won't know how long it will actually take you to teach a unit until you teach it. The actual start and end dates will most likely change. What plotting does is give you a game plan. Remember, when plotting your units, to consider the importance of continuity. For example, you wouldn't want to start a unit on a day before a special event (such as prom day, track-and-field day, yearbook day), the day before a holiday, or the day before students will be out of class for an extended period of time (such as for standardized testing) and expect they will come back with the same enthusiasm for their studies. For the same reason, you wouldn't want to begin a new unit on a Friday.

Note: Make sure you are familiar with the skills and concepts being tested on the standardized tests required by your school or state, and teach the units that focus on those skills and concepts prior to the administration of the tests. Remember, it is your responsibility to prepare your students to do well on those exams.

 *P*lanning Units of Instruction

Once you have identified the units you will be teaching, you are ready to begin laying out the content you want to cover in each unit. In doing so, consider the following:

1. How you want to organize your unit (that is, chronologically, thematically, sequentially, or another way).

2. What instructional goals will be addressed in the unit.
   Note: Instructional goals are learning competencies that students are expected to achieve. To ensure compliance with the federal No Child Left Behind (NCLB) Act, most schools are using state and national standards as their target instructional goals. It is not necessary that you teach to all the state and national competencies in every unit; however, you will be expected that you address all of them over the course of the year.

3. What instructional objectives are going to be addressed in the unit.
   Note: Instructional objectives are measurable behavioral expectations that support the unit instructional goals. They identify exactly what students will know and be able to do at the end of the unit.
   Note: Instructional goals are learning outcomes that are expressed in general terms and reflect the "big picture," whereas instructional objectives are learning outcomes that are specifically identified, such as the following:

   Instructional goal: To provide opportunities for students to listen, read, write, think, and speak critically (New Jersey State Department of Education, Core Curriculum Standards 3.1, 3.2, 3.3).
   Instructional objective: To read "A Fool's Paradise" and identify themes, patterns of imagery, symbolism, and character motivations.

4. What type of assessment tool you want to use to identify your students' instructional needs. (See Chapter 4 for suggestions.)

5. What texts are going to be used to meet the goals and instructional objectives. Units should contain a wide range of materials, including texts (textbooks, novels, short stories, plays, poetry, lyrics, nonfiction accounts, news and magazine articles), film, musical selections, artifacts, graphs, charts, pictures, computer programs, guest speakers, class trips, documents, experiments, models, interviews, surveys, presentations, etc.

6. How much time you are going to assign to each text. There are no hard-and-set rules about time. Curriculum guides typically provide estimated time frames, but these are just estimates. Two different classes taught the same lesson by the same teacher could, because of student differences, conceivably take different lengths of time to complete. If you do not have a guide to follow, good resources for time frames are content area supervisors and teachers who have either taught the course or taught the students who will be in your class. Another source is lessons in your content area that are available online. Reviewing a few of these will give you an idea of how much time other teachers are taking to cover similar material. (See Model 11: Lesson Plan for

suggestions.) Once you have taught your first unit and have become familiar with the pace of your students' learning as well as the pace of your teaching, you will have a realistic basis for timing the rest of your units. In general, it is better to overplan than to underplan. Unit and lesson plans should be seen as flexible guidelines. Multiple modifications and revisions throughout the year are anticipated and expected.

7. Identify how you plan to assess your students' learning. Remember that units must include multiple forms of assessments. (See Chapter 4 for suggestions.)

8. Evaluate your unit to ensure you have included all the necessary components.

9. Decide the order in which you want to teach the texts.

10. Develop daily lesson plans to support unit goals and objectives. (See Model 10: Unit Plan.)

*P*lanning Unit Lessons

Lesson planning is all about decision making, creativity, and passion for your discipline. It's where you get to use your expertise to make critical choices that will empower students with not only an understanding but also hopefully with an interest in your content area that will continue beyond your classroom. While the instructional goals are determined for you, how you help your students reach those goals is in your hands. You get to select and sequence the texts, strategies, activities, assignments, and assessments that will literally bring what they're learning to life for them.

Step 1. Note the theme or focus of the unit.

Step 2. Identify the unit instructional goals the lesson will be supporting.

Step 3. Identify the texts you will be using for the lesson.

Step 4. Identify the instructional objectives of the lesson. Remember, instructional objectives are lesson specific and must be measurable. For example, "students will enjoy the story" is certainly a desirable outcome, but because it cannot be measured it would not be a suitable instructional objective.

Step 5. Identify the learning-style focus of this lesson. Most teachers tend to use strategies that are compatible with their own learning style, which is fine for the students who share the same learning style but disastrous for students who learn differently. (See Chapter 4.) Noting the learning styles addressed on each lesson plan will help you see gaps in your instructional strategies, which need to be addressed in order to accommodate the learning needs of *all* the students in your class.

   Note: It is unrealistic to assume that all learning styles will be addressed in every lesson; however, all the learning styles of your students should be given consideration over the course of the unit. Knowing the learning styles of the students in your classroom and being aware of the styles addressed in the lesson will alert you to disconnects and identify for you the students who may have difficulty meeting the expectations of the lesson. Knowing this in advance, you can prepare to assist these students with differentiated strategies so that they too can be successful.

Step 6. Identify how you are going to teach to the goals and objectives—the lesson. Cohesive lessons are presented in three parts: the introduction, learning activities, and closure.

- A strong *introduction*, which makes the immediate connection between the students and what they are going to learn, will pique your students' interest and make them want to participate in the activities that follow. The best introductions help the students personally connect with the subject matter, giving it relevance and meaning, which will translate for them into a reason to learn.

   Examples of weak introductions
   a. "Students, turn to page 14 in your books and begin reading about the beach."
   b. "Today we are going to study the beach."

   Examples of strong introductions (early grades)
   a. Bring in a tape of the sounds of the beach and ask students what they hear or what it reminds them of.
   b. Hold up a picture of a beach scene and ask students to tell you what they see, what they hear, what they smell.
   c. For students who have never been to the beach, bring in a bucket of sand and a bucket of dirt and bottles of salt and fresh water. Let the students touch and smell the sand, dirt, and water so that they can tell you the differences and similarities. Bring in seashells and pictures of sea creatures and ask them to match the sea creatures to the shells and tell you the criteria they used to make the matches. Ask them to tell you what the shells tell them about what life must be like under the sea.
   d. Show students a clip from a movie or television show with a beach scene and ask them what they see and hear and what inferences they can make

about people who like or dislike the beach or ask them what they like or dislike about the beach.

e. Ask them to think about what it would be like to live on the beach or ask them to tell you what they think the pros and cons of living on the beach would be. What makes going to the beach fun? What takes away from the fun?

f. Use K-W-L (Ogle, 1986): A strategy that asks students to identify what they know (K), what they want to know (W) about a topic before they begin their reading, and then what they learned (L). (See Chapter 6.)

Examples of strong introductions (6–12)

a. Give students a prompt related to the subject matter of the lesson and five minutes to respond in their journals. This will give them an opportunity to identify and formulate their opinions on the topic before they are asked to share them.

b. Ask a provocative question that will connect the students personally with the subject (e.g., Has anyone here ever witnessed an act of prejudice either inside or outside of school?).

c. Show a clip from a movie or television show dealing with the same subject and ask for reactions.

d. Present a scenario and ask the students in small groups to come up with a solution or tell you how they would have handled the same situation.

e. Share a recent newspaper article or clip of a newscaster reporting on a situation similar to one you'll be considering in your lesson.

f. Use K-W-L, which is equally effective with students in the upper grades.

- A list of *activities* tells what your students will do during the lesson. Next to each activity, identify the learning style being addressed.

- The *closure*, like the introduction, is equally important as the lesson itself. It is in this part of the lesson that you help students make sense of the activities. You can't assume that students will see the "big picture" and make connections on their own. You must help them understand the usefulness or meaning of what they have just learned. A good idea is to literally ask them how what they have learned can be seen in or applied to their lives outside of the classroom.

Step 7. Identify the student's homework assignment. The purpose of homework is to reinforce skills and concepts taught in the lesson. Therefore, the homework assignment should always be directly related to the content of the lesson. It is another way for you to assess whether your students have understood what was taught in the lesson. Reviewing homework will inform you of the skills and concepts that need more attention before you move on to the next lesson. For this reason, it is important that the homework be given attention the next day.

Note: Never use homework as punishment. It is also important that when you are assigning homework you be sensitive to the amount of time it will take students to finish the assignment. Remember, students have already spent six to seven hours in a classroom. Asking younger students to spend another two to three hours on homework is unreasonable. An easy way to check to see if the amount of homework you're assigning is reasonable is to ask students and/or their parents how much time is being spent on homework each evening. You can be sure they will greatly appreciate your intuitiveness and sensitivity.

Step 8. Identify the materials or equipment you will need for the lesson. If you need special materials, supplies, or equipment that are not normally housed in your classroom, order or reserve what you need for that day at least a week or two in advance. Ask your supervisor at the beginning of the school year what the procedures and time lines are for ordering and reserving. There is nothing worse for teachers than to have a great lesson and not have the resources to teach it because they were remiss in scheduling equipment or ordering materials.

Step 9. Identify how you are going to assess whether your students understand the skills and concepts taught in this lesson. Students run into trouble when their teachers move ahead to the next lesson before they have had an opportunity to master the skills and concepts taught in the previous lesson. Assess students' mastery at the conclusion of each lesson to prevent this from happening. See Model 11: Lesson Plan.

Note: Asking students if they understand is not a viable assessment tool. Many times students *think* they understand when they really don't. For that reason, you need to use an assessment tool that accurately identifies and documents your students' learning. (See Chapter 4 for suggestions.)

Step 10. It is important that at the end of each lesson, you take the time to review your lesson and the performance of both you and your students. Understand and accept that becoming an exemplary teacher doesn't happen overnight. The best teachers are those who are constantly reflecting, self-evaluating, and looking for ways to improve their teaching. An easy way to monitor your lessons and teaching is with a self-assessment tool that can be personalized, duplicated, and placed in your unit binder at the end of each lesson. You will find these extremely helpful when you review and modify your units for use the following year. See Model 12: Teacher Reflection and Self-Assessment.

Online Resources

Over time, you begin to develop a teaching style that will be entirely your own. The way you interact with students, the way you move about the classroom, the way you look at students and communicate nonverbally, the way you use the tone and inflections of your voice to articulate and accentuate ideas, the way you question students, and the way you pace your lessons are all characteristically unique. No two teachers are exactly the same. For that reason, you should not expect that you could use another teacher's lesson plans and get the same results. You will find that teaching from plans that are taken verbatim from books or websites will be less satisfying because they will not be entirely compatible with your teaching style. You should, however, look at other teachers' plans to see what they are thinking and doing. There are places online, for example, that you can go to get ideas that you could modify to accommodate your teaching style and incorporate into your own plans. Table 3.2 lists websites that you should consider visiting.

Planning for English Language Learners

If you have English language learners (ELLs) in your class, you will have the additional responsibility of teaching content skills and concepts to "English language learners in strategic ways that make the concepts comprehensible while promoting the students' academic English language development" (Short & Echevarria, 2004/2005, p. 10). Without question, this is a formidable task, especially for teachers who have limited experience with languages and cultures other than their own. You can, however, take steps that will help you meet this challenge. The first is to make ELL accommodations an integral part of your planning process.

This process should begin with the collection of information about your students. Research showed us early on that when students' first language is valued

Table 3.2 Websites for Lesson Models and Ideas

Discipline	Website
Art (visual and performance)	www.lessonplanspage.com www.teacher.scholastic.com www.mcrel.org/lesson-plans www.bestwebquests.com www.smithsonianeducation.org/educators
Economics	www.mcrel.org/lesson-plans www.bestwebquests.com
English/Language Arts/Reading	www.lessonplanspage.com www.teacher.scholastic.com www.mcrel.org/lesson-plans www.bestwebquests.com
Foreign Languages	www.mcrel.org/lesson-plans www.bestwebquests.com www.nwrel.org/sky/index.php www.eduref.org
Geography	www.nationalgeographic.education.com www.mcrel.org/lesson-plans
Health	www.lessonplanspage.com www.teacher.scholastic.com www.mcrel.org/lesson-plans www.nwrel.org/sky/index.php
History/Civics/Social Studies	www.civiced.org www.lessonplanspage.com www.teacher.scholastic.com www.mcrel.org/lesson-plans www.bestwebquests.com www.smithsonianeducation.org/educators
Mathematics	www.nctm.org www.lessonplanspage.com www.teacher.scholastic.com www.mcrel.org/lesson-plans www.bestwebquests.com
Physical Education	www.teacher.scholastic.com www.mcrel.org/lesson-plans www.nwrel.org/sky/index.php
Psychology	www.eduref.org/cgi-bin/lessons.cgi/social_studies/psychology

(continued)

Table 3.2, *Continued*

Discipline	Website
Science	www.lessonplanspage.com
	www.teacher.scholastic.com
	www.mcrel.org/lesson-plans
	www.bestwebquests.com
	www.smithsonianeducation.org/educators
Technology	www.lessonplanspage.com
	www.teacher.scholastic.com
	www.mcrel.org/lesson-plans
	www.smithsonianeducation.org/educators
	www.bestwebquests.com

and fostered ELLs are more successful academically because they are allowed and encouraged to call on their established knowledge base and personal experiences to support their learning (Hakuta, 1986). For this reason, it is important to consider student backgrounds and interests when planning lessons. If you provide ELLs with specific examples from schema they understand, they have a better chance of understanding new concepts. This will require that you spend time talking to them (either one on one or through an interpreter) to collect information that you can use to plan your lessons. When planning, make it a practice to do the following:

1. Incorporate an *explicit* ELL vocabulary component into your daily plans, which will provide students with the language they will need to navigate the lesson (that is, content-related vocabulary; directional words such as *compare, contrast, dissect, support, argue,* etc.; colloquial expressions you may use in your teaching). An easy way to determine language beyond the content that students will need is to tape-record a few of your classes and note the kind of language and language patterns you tend to use when teaching.

2. Present key concepts in multiple modes so that ELLs can "learn by seeing concepts demonstrated, by hearing them described, and by participating in activities that show the concepts in action" (Carrier, 2006, p. 131).

3. Include *explicit* language objectives (reading, writing, speaking, viewing, etc.) for ELLs in all your lessons.

4. Plan activities that will give students opportunities to extend their academic talk both individually and in groups.

5. Plan support for each lesson (e.g., anticipation guides, visual aids, vocabulary lists with definitions, chapter outlines) that students can be given in advance of the lesson so that they can prepare to learn.

*P*utting Planning into Perspective

The necessity for unit and lesson planning should be clear. Academically and pedagogically sound plans legitimize your practices, while providing purpose, direction, and focus to your teaching. Walking into a classroom without a well-thought-out lesson plan is like a coach sending his or her team onto the field without a game plan. The probability that either of you will come home a winner is not great.

*R*eferences

Carrier, K. (January/February 2006). Improving comprehension and assessment of English language learners using MMIO. *The Clearing House, 79*(3), 131–136.

Hakuta, K. (1986). *Mirror of language*. New York: Basic Books.

New Jersey State Department of Education. (Fall 1998). *New Jersey core curriculum content standards*. Retrieved January 2, 2006, from www.state.nj.us/njded/cccs/

No Child Left Behind Act, § 20 U.S.C. 6301 et seq.

Ogle, D. M. (1986). K-W-L: A teaching model that develops active reading of expository text. *The Reading Teacher, 39*(6), 564–570.

Short, D., & Echevarria, J. (December 2004/January 2005). Teacher skills to support English language learners. *Educational Leadership, 62*(4), 8–13.

*O*nline References

PBS Teachers—www.pbs.org/teachers

Moodle—http://moodle.org

Teacher Resources—www.learnReturn.com

A-Z Teacher Stuff—www.atozteacherstuff.com/Model 13

Unit Plan

Unit: Things are not always the way they appear. **Grade:** 9 Language Arts

Learning Styles: Visual, verbal, auditory, independent, social, applied

Instructional Goals:

1. Provide opportunities for students to listen, read, write, think, and speak critically (New Jersey State Department of Education, Core Curriculum Standards 3.1, 3.2, 3.3).
2. Provide opportunities for students to critically read and respond to a variety of texts (New Jersey State Department of Education Core Curriculum Standards 3.4, 3.5).

Instructional Objectives: At the end of this unit, students should be able to

a. understand the difference between appearance and reality.

b. analyze character actions for motivations.

c. evaluate advertisements for credibility.

d. begin understanding the following literary terms: theme, symbol, image.

e. contribute meaningfully to discussions within groups.

f. write a cohesive essay.

g. respond to objective questions designed to test reading comprehension.

h. critically respond to their readings with journal entries.

i. expand their vocabulary with twenty new words from their reading.

Pre-teaching Assessment Tool: *T* or *F* inventory on literary terms and concepts developed in the unit.

Texts:

a. Nonfiction: "A Fool's Paradise" by Floyd Dell

b. Poetry: "A War Prayer" by Edgar Allan Poe

c. Film: *Murder, She Wrote*, starring Angela Lansbury

d. Advertisements from magazines and television commercials

e. Fiction: *A Separate Peace* by John Knowles

f. Film: *A Separate Peace*

g. Artifact: Body biographies (*A Separate Peace* characters)

h. Graphics: Survey and graph of perceptions of betrayal

Estimated Time Frame: 30 Days

a. "A Fool's Paradise"	3 days
b. "A War Prayer"	2 days
c. *Murder, She Wrote*	5 days
d. Advertisements	5 days
e. *A Separate Peace*	15 days

Teaching Strategies:

a. Reader Responses	f. Journals
b. Surveys	g. Open-ended questioning
c. Q&A	h. Body biographies
d. Student presentations	i. Read-alouds
e. Direct instruction	j. Journal responses

Assessments:

a. Participation in Reader Response groups	f. Objective reading quizzes
b. Essay responses	g. Student-teacher conferences
c. Journal responses	h. Homework responses
d. Analysis of survey responses	i. Responses to direct questioning
e. Teacher observations	j. Student presentations

Lesson Plan

Title of Unit: Things are not always as they appear.   **Grade:** 9   **Time Frame:** 2 days

Learning-Style Focus: auditory, social, verbal

Text(s): Print: "A Fool's Paradise"

Instructional Goals: To provide opportunities for students to listen, read, write, think, and speak critically (New Jersey State Department of Education, Core Curriculum Standards 3.1, 3.2, 3.3).

Instructional Objectives: Students should be able to
1. read "A Fool's Paradise" critically and understand the difference between appearance and reality.
2. identify theme.
3. identify character motivations.
4. make predictions based on textual information.
5. understand the meaning of *respectability, deceptive, evasion, comparative, immaculate, currency, arrogant, anxiety, bewilderment, renunciation,* and *tendrils.*
6. write responses to text in their journals.
7. talk about the text in response groups.

Lesson:

Introduction: Students will be asked to respond to the following prompt in their response journals: Do you think your parents should always tell you the truth or are there times when you think it is acceptable for them to keep the truth from you?

Activities: [Next to each activity, identify the learning style(s) addressed.]
1. Q&A: Students, in pairs, will listen to me read the first paragraph. At the end of the paragraph, students will each write one question that they have about the events in the first paragraph. Students will then ask their partners the question and record the answer given. Questions and answers will be shared with the rest of the class. This activity will be repeated with the rest of the story. (verbal, auditory, social)
2. Students will return to their response groups to collectively consider the following questions: (auditory, social, verbal)
   a. What decisions made by the parents were good ones? Which ones were bad?
   b. How was the boy helped by their decisions? How was he hurt?
   c. Should the boy have been told the truth? Why or why not?
3. Students will share group opinions with the class.

Closure: Teacher-led discussion: What do you think the author was trying to tell us through this story? Can you see that there was a difference between the way things appeared and the way they actually were? How can you see this being helpful in your own lives?

Homework Assignment:
In your journals, make a list of ways you predict the decisions of the parents will affect the boy in the future. Next to the effect, explain why you think this might happen. (independent, verbal)

Materials Needed: Paper, pens, short story "A Fool's Paradise"

Assessment: Student understanding will be assessed by (1) meaningful participation in share-pair and response groups and (2) written responses in journal.

Reflection/Self-Assessment:

Teacher Reflection and Self-Assessment

Lesson: _____ Date: _____

1. What went well, and why? _____
_____
_____
_____

2. What didn't go well, and why? _____
_____
_____
_____

3. Which instructional objectives were met? _____
_____
_____
_____

4. Which instructional objectives were not met? _____
_____
_____
_____

5. Which students had difficulty with the lesson? _____
_____
_____
_____

6. Which students had no difficulty with the lesson? _____
_____
_____
_____

7. What can I do to improve the lesson? _____
_____
_____
_____

Evaluating Student Knowledge and Performance

*H*ow Student Evaluation Has Changed

The past twenty years have witnessed significant philosophical and pedagogical changes in our thinking about *how* we measure, *what* we measure, *when* we measure, and *why* we measure student competencies. Arguably, the most significant change has been in *how we measure* student learning, which has pedagogically moved from exclusively administering objective tests to following an evaluative process that has been redefined to include assessment, evaluation, grading, and application.

Step 1. Assessment is the process by which information about student learning is gathered. To accommodate student differences in learning styles and to ensure an accurate and a balanced appraisal of student knowledge, understanding, and abilities, a wide range of assessment tools must be used, which includes traditional testing as well as alternate forms of assessment (such as performances, projects, teacher observations).

Step 2. Evaluation is the process of interpreting the information gathered on the assessments. This is typically done with rubrics, which identify and clarify learning and performance goals.

Step 3. Grading is the process of assigning a quantitative value to the evaluations. Grades are an important step in this process because they give us a systematic way to visualize, discuss, and compare student progress in relationship to previous assessments, to other students' performance on assessments, and to state and national standards.

Step 4. Application is the process of taking the results of the assessments and using them to monitor current practices and to inform future instruction (individual and/or whole class).

What we measure has also changed significantly. While objective tests measured what students recalled, they didn't account for students' understandings or for their ability to apply what they knew. Therefore, evaluations had to be modified to include the measurement of student comprehension, which, in order to provide a more accurate and comprehensive view of student learning, required the use of alternate evaluative instruments (e.g., performance, portfolios, projects) in addition to traditional objective testing.

When we measure, like our belief in what should be measured, has also changed dramatically. Traditionally, teachers tested student learning at the end of the lesson or unit taught. Once the tests were administered and scored, the teachers moved on to their next set of lessons. This was fine for the students who did well on the tests; however, for the students who did poorly, this presented problems, particularly if the information tested was necessary for them to understand the skills and concepts being taught in the units that followed. These students were essentially doomed to fail. To prevent this from happening, teachers now are encouraged to administer a wide range of assessments throughout the unit. These ongoing assessments help teachers identify student misunderstandings so they can be corrected before the student fails.

Our understanding of *why we measure* has also changed. At one time, assessments were used exclusively to identify and validate learning and to determine student placement. After reviewing the assessments with the students, they were typically filed and only used, if needed, to clarify grades to interested parents and administrators. No longer filed away, assessment tools are now used by teachers to inform their instruction. Assessments identify very quickly for teachers which students need additional tutorial support and what skill and concept misunderstandings need further attention prior to moving on to the next unit of instruction.

Types of Assessments

Table 4.1 lists some of the tools you can use to assess your students' learning. It is important that your assessment be ongoing and varied enough to account for all of the learning styles of the students in your classroom.

Table 4.1 Types of Assessments

Assessment	Characteristics	Examples
Summative	Given at the end of the unit to measure student learning. Always graded.	Objective and subjective exams, reports, projects.
Formative	Given periodically during the learning experience to identify student progress and identify student misunderstandings and errors so that they can be corrected prior to the summative assessments. Can be graded, but need not be.	Quizzes, graphic organizers, worksheets, interviews, conferences, student questioning, rough drafts.
Norm-referenced	Based on standards, compares students with other students in the same grade level.	State and national standardized tests, SAT, Iowa Test of Basic Skills.
Authentic	Mirrors kinds of activities students experience outside the classroom.	Presentations, performances, experiments, inventions, conferences, interviews, surveys, debates, exhibitions.
Text-based	Developed directly from curriculum-based texts.	Essays, objective quizzes and exams.
Teacher-developed	Developed by teachers to supplement information from authentic and text-based assessments.	Essays, objective quizzes and exams, research projects, graphic organizers.

(continued)

Table 4.1, Continued

Assessment	Characteristics	Examples
Computer-based	Developed by computer companies to reinforce classroom learning, skill- and concept-based, providing more complex questions as the student responds correctly.	Tutorials, skill and concept drills.
Portfolios	Collection of pieces of representative individual student work.	Collection of student products (essays, poems, art, music, etc.).
Teacher observations	Observations of students engaged in classroom activities. Can be academic or behavioral. Recorded, dated, and used to clarify student needs or behavior.	See Model 17: Teacher Observation Form.
Teacher questioning	Used to assess student knowledge and understanding.	Literal and probative questions about readings, experiences, and applications.
Peer reviews	Using a rubric, peers evaluate specific aspects of each other's work.	Edit or evaluate peer work (writings, presentations, artwork, performances).
Self-assessment	Using self-assessment tools, students evaluate their own learning and learning needs.	Journals, learning logs, self-evaluation forms. See Model 19: Self-Evaluation Form.

Selecting Appropriate Assessments

Before you begin the process of designing an assessment, you must first identify exactly what you want to know and what each type of assessment can tell you about your students' learning. (See Table 4.2.)

When selecting assessments, think in terms of units of instruction. Use the following checklist to ensure fair, complete, and accurate assessment of your students' knowledge and understanding. Each unit should include assessments that

____ Are ongoing, purposeful, and meaningful.

____ Reflect what has been taught.

____ Tell you what students know, what they understand, and how they relate what they know and understand to the world outside the classroom.

Table 4.2 Assessment Chart

Assessment Goal	What Assessment Measures	Examples	Assessment Tool
To assess content knowledge and information	Students' ability to recall objective information and data (what, when, where, how)	Formulas, spelling, definitions, grammar facts, details, rules, addition and multiplication tables	Objective tests/quizzes, summaries, retellings, worksheets, researched reports, book reports, oral presentations, computer-assisted programs
To assess comprehension	Students' understandings based on objective data and information (why)	Cause and effect, character motivations, relationships, implications, interpretations	Essays, graphic organizers, Reader Response groups, learning logs, projects, presentations, inventions, journals, analytical research papers, debates
To assess transference of knowledge	Students' ability to apply the data and their understandings to life outside the classroom (application)	Activities mirroring life outside the classroom	Portfolios, presentations, inventions, conferences, interviews, surveys, performances, original writings, exhibitions
To assess reading (K–4)	Students' reading levels, decoding skills, and reading behaviors	Miscues, omits words, substitutes words, self-corrects, asks for help	Running records, anecdotal records, retelling, developmental checklists
To assess student perceptions	How students perceive what they know, what they need to know, and what they want to know	Student's belief that he or she has understanding, which may or may not be true	Learning logs, journals, teacher questioning, student-teacher conferences

____ Align with the goals and objectives of the lesson and unit.

____ Align with state and national standards.

____ Use multiple texts (novels, poetry, drama, short stories, nonfiction, documents, film, television, newspapers, computer programs, audio, surveys, interviews, class trips, etc.).

____ Require students to use multiple strategies (writing, speaking, listening and responding, performing, drawing, interpreting, reviewing, building, etc.).

___ Allow for a variety of responses (objective, interpretative, authentic).

___ Correspond to student learning styles.

___ Include opportunities for students to self-assess.

___ Provide information about student learning that you can use to monitor and evaluate your own teaching.

Developing Effective Test Questions

Objective Tests (Multiple Choice, True/False, Matching, Fill in the Blank)

An objective test is one that requires no judgment by the scorer when it is being marked. The most important attribute of an objective test is *content validity*, which exists when the test measures what the teacher wants it to measure; that is, the questions match a set of predetermined objectives. A second important attribute of an objective test is *reliability*, or consistency. A reliable test is one that would produce similar results if it were administered again to a similar group of students. Objective testing has both advantages and disadvantages as noted in the following list:

Advantages

Tests can be used to measure a broad content area.

Tests can measure thought-process levels, from recall to critical thinking.

Tests are highly reliable. Scoring standards are fixed.

Tests can be machine scored.

Disadvantages

Tests are time consuming to construct.

Students' responses are subject to guessing. Teachers don't know if a right answer is a result of knowledge or a lucky guess.

Slow or weak readers operate at a disadvantage.

Tests cannot assess students' ability to write.

Guidelines for Developing Multiple-Choice Questions

Multiple-choice questions typically provide students with a stem (a complete or partial question or statement) and four response choices that will make the information in the stem true or accurate.

- Ask significant questions that reflect students' understanding and knowledge.
- State the question clearly and concisely in the stem so that students know what the question is asking.
- Order the responses in a logical way.
- Avoid putting grammatical clues to the answer in the stem.
- Avoid giving 3/1 or 4/1 splits in responses where one response is overtly different from the others.
- Avoid using "all of the above" or "none of the above."
- Provide responses that are uniform in length.
- Make all of the responses plausible.
- Make choices parallel in structure.
- Try to avoid a negative format in the questions.
- Provide one clear answer.
- Randomize the position of the correct answers.

Adapted from *The AP Vertical Teams Guide for English*, 2002. New York: College Entrance Examination Board.

Examples of common errors made in writing multiple-choice questions

1. Asking questions that provide no insights into what the student knows about content.

   Example: The author's first name is
   A. Sam   C. Bruce
   B. Alex   D. John

2. Providing answers that are absurd and obviously incorrect.

   Example: The word *limpid* has the same meaning as the word
   A. cold   C. stupid
   B. clear   D. snowy

3. Putting grammatical clues in the stem.

   Example: The words "Lolling dogs droop in dead doorways" are an example of an
   A. alliteration   C. simile
   B. metonymy   D. pun

4. Writing questions that are unclear, lacking enough information in the stem for students to understand what is being asked.

   Example: The character is
   A. unhappy   C. successful
   B. intelligent   D. creative

5. Providing answers that are obvious 3/1 or 4/1 splits, where one answer is completely different from the others.

   Example: The tone of the first stanza of the poem is
   A. calm   C. joyful
   B. casual   D. exhausting

6. Providing answers that differ in length.

   Example: The phrase "dead doorways" implies that buildings are
   A. very hot   C. cool
   B. locked   D. deserted and totally empty of all life

Guidelines for Developing True/False Tests

True/false tests are relatively easy to construct, administer, and score. Keep in mind the following four things when developing the questions:

1. Make sure the questions are worth asking.

   Example: What is the author's middle name? is not worth asking.

2. Write the questions clearly and concisely; avoid unnecessary language.

   Example: In the question, *Thomas Jefferson was a wealthy landowner who wrote the Declaration of Independence*, the first part of the question is unnecessary.

3. Make sure each question is either clearly true or clearly false.

   Example: Farmers are given subsidies by the government.

   Explanation: Although some farmers are given subsidies, not all are, making the question sometimes true and sometimes false, but not clearly either true or false.

4. Don't mix facts in the question.

   Example: A square is a <u>geometric shape</u> that has <u>three sides</u>.
                                     Fact 1   Fact 2

Guidelines for Developing Matching Tests

A matching test consists of two lists of items. These exams are used by teachers to test their students' ability to see *relationships* between the items in the two lists. The following is important when developing a matching test:

1. A clear relationship must exist between the two lists (such as causes and effects, novels and characters, tools and their uses, terms and definitions, problems and solutions).

2. The directions must clarify the relationship between the two lists.

3. One list should be longer than the other to encourage reasoning rather than the process of elimination.

Guidelines for Developing Fill-in-the-Blank Tests

Fill-ins require that students use textual clues and recall as well their understanding of the material world and reasoning skills to answer the questions correctly. When developing fill-in-the-blank tests, you need to do the following:

1. Indicate in the directions if more than one answer could satisfy the question.

2. Include questions that assess students' comprehension as well as their ability to recall details.

   Example: Jane was angry with her father because _____.

3. Provide enough information in the stem to enable the students to answer the question.

   Poor: _____ went _____ to find _____.

   Better: Directly following play practice, Sally went _____ to find _____.

4. Structure the sentence so that the appropriate word when placed in the blank will make the sentence grammatically correct.

   Poor: Following his trip abroad, Sam suffered from an *rare* disease.

   Better: Following his trip abroad, Sam suffered from a *rare* disease.

Subjective Tests (Essay Exams)

Subjective tests require that scorers use their judgment when marking the tests. There's not always a "right" answer and, like objective exams, they have advantages and disadvantages associated with them.

Advantages	Disadvantages
Tests are relatively easy to construct.	Reliability of scoring tends to be low.
Tests can examine a topic in depth.	Tests can be laborious to score.
Tests give students an opportunity to show what they know.	Students with weak writing skills are disadvantaged.
Tests can assess students' ability to reason and write.	Tests measure a limited content sample.

Guidelines for Developing Essay Tests

- Ask significant questions that reflect what has been taught.

- Ask students to develop an *in-depth* response to only *one* idea.

- Remind students that responses require a topic paragraph with a thesis statement, supportive paragraphs, and a concluding paragraph. *Note:* Short answers are not essays!

- Include exam directions that require students to support their opinions with specific examples from their texts, their learned knowledge, or their experiences.

- Limit questions enough to be answered in-depth within the testing period. (Rule of thumb: one question per 45-minute period.)

- Build time into the testing period for students to organize and edit their responses.

- Provide students with an essay format prior to the test. (Teachers primarily interested in responses permit students to have a copy of the format on their desks during testing.)

- Use test-specific rubrics to score exams to ensure scoring reliability. (See Figure 4.1.)

Figure 4.1

Rubric for Scoring Writing Assignments (Grades 4–5)

Name: _____ Date: _____

Class: _____ Assignment: _____

Skill	Excellent (3)	Good (2)	Needs Improvement (1)	Score
Topic Paragraph	Topic paragraph is well developed and includes summary details and a main idea.	Topic paragraph has summary details and main idea but needs to be developed with more information.	Topic paragraph is missing summary details and main idea, or needs to be developed with more information.	
Supporting Paragraphs				
Topic Sentences	All of the topic sentences support the main idea.	Most of the topic sentences support the main idea.	Most of the topic sentences do not support the main idea.	
Supporting Sentences	All of the sentences support the paragraph topic sentence.	Most of the sentences support the paragraph topic sentence.	Most of the sentences do not support the paragraph topic sentence.	
Concluding Sentences	All paragraphs have concluding sentences.	One paragraph is missing a concluding sentence.	More than one paragraph is missing a concluding sentence.	
Concluding Paragraph	Paragraph summarizes the main ideas in paper.	Paragraph summarizes most main ideas.	Paragraph is missing or fails to summarize main ideas.	
Content	Content has three excellent ideas that support the main idea.	Content has three good ideas that support the main idea.	Content has fewer than three good ideas or has errors in information presented.	
Neatness	Paper has margins and is neat.	Paper has margins, but may have some marks.	Paper is missing margins and/or is messy.	
Organization	Ideas are presented in a logical order.	Most of the ideas are presented in a logical order.	Ideas are not presented in an organized way.	
Spelling and Word Usage	All of the words are used correctly without any spelling errors.	Most of the words are used correctly. There may be one spelling error.	The errors in word usage and/or spelling make reading and understanding difficult.	
Capitalization	Capital letters are used appropriately.	There may be one capitalization error.	More than one error in capitalization exists.	
Sentence Structure	All of the sentences are complete and correctly structured.	Most of the sentences are complete and correctly structured.	Many sentences are incomplete and/or incorrectly structured.	
Total Score				

Scoring: A=30–33; B=26–29; C=22–25; D=19–21
Comments/Suggestions:

Types of Essay Questions

- *Closed-ended questions* are those in which the teacher has predetermined what information is expected to be found in the answer—for example, "Identify and describe five different ways we use water in our community."

- *Open-ended questions* are those that allow students to use their own thoughts, reasons, and experiences, in addition to textual knowledge, in the answer. They have no predetermined "correct" answer. Open-ended questions ask students to make connections between what they have learned and their own lives. *Note:* Personalizing the question makes it more understandable and easier for students to respond to. For example, instead of asking students "What would it be like to be blind?" ask "If you suddenly lost your sight, how would your life change?"

Developing Good Essay Questions

Keep the following in mind when writing essay questions:

1. Keep the question simple. Be clear and concise. Avoid unnecessary language that may confuse students' understanding of what is being asked.

    Poor: Write a descriptive essay concerning the functionality of computers.

    Better: Describe the different ways computers are used today.

2. Include directional words in the question that will clarify what students need to do (*compare, contrast, identify, describe, defend, refute, explain, support, clarify,* etc.).

    Example: Defend or refute the idea that countries benefit from war. Give reasons and examples from history to support your position.

3. Clearly identify any specific information you want in the response.

    Example: Describe the major contributions President Richard Nixon made while in the White House. Include specific examples of political, economic, and social contributions in your essay.

4. Limit the question to make answering it possible within the testing period.

    Poor: Discuss the Civil War.

    Better: Identify the major events that led up to the Civil War and explain the significance of each event.

5. Include only ideas directly related to the main idea of the question.

Poor: Identify the major themes in *Death of a Salesman* and explain why you chose them and in what other texts you have seen them.

Better: Identify the major themes in *Death of a Salesman*. Give specific examples in the play to support your opinions.

Note: When developing tests, it's always a good idea to take the test yourself before giving it to your students. This way, if there are any problems with the questions, you can sort them out before they become major problems on test day.

Making Sense of Subjective Assessments

One of the problems that new teachers frequently have is how to translate subjective assessments, once they have them, into usable information that they can call on to support their students' learning and to validate their own subsequent curricular decisions. For many, developing interesting assignments that are also creative and provocative is the easy part. The difficult part is to figure out a way of grading the assignments that is fair and consistent with the goals and objectives of the assignment itself. The solution to this problem is to develop and use rubrics. A *rubric* is a set of criteria that identifies the expectations for a completed product. "Rubrics require a Likert-type scale to quantify decisions about performance and a semantic scale to describe different levels of learning for a particular activity" (Stanford & Reeves, 2005, p. 18). Rubrics do the following:

- Eliminate confusion for students by explicitly identifying the knowledge and performance expectations of the assignment.
- Simplify the grading process by focusing the evaluator's attention on specific information and skills.
- Objectify the evaluation by assigning competency levels (1–3) to specific outcomes.
- Ensure that all student work is evaluated in the same way, which eliminates real or imagined teacher biases.
- Visually display student strengths and weaknesses, which makes for easy monitoring for both students and teachers.
- Provide a quick and easy way to check the alignment of the assignment to lesson/unit and/or state and national standards.

Figure 4.2

Rubric for Scoring Analytical Writing

Name: _____   Date: _____

Assignment: _____

Category	Excellent (3)	Adequate (2)	Unacceptable (1)	Score
Title Page	Correctly structured.	Title page has minor errors in form and structure.	N/A	
Introduction and Conclusion	The paper has a strong introduction and conclusion.	The paper includes a weak introduction and/or conclusion.	The paper is missing either an introduction or a conclusion.	
Topic Sentences	All supportive paragraphs have topic sentences that support the thesis.	N/A	Most topic sentences do not support the thesis.	
Supporting Sentences	All supportive examples are complete and support the topic sentence.	Most of the supportive examples are complete and support the topic sentence.	Supportive examples are incomplete and/or do not support the topic sentence.	
Paragraph Explanations	All paragraph explanations clearly explain how the example supports the topic sentence.	Most of the paragraph explanations clearly explain how the example supports the topic sentence.	Paragraph explanations do not clearly explain how the example supports the topic sentence.	
Completeness of Response	The paper has five supporting paragraphs.	N/A	The paper is missing supporting paragraphs.	
Tenses	All of the verbs are in proper tense.	Errors in tense are not excessive.	Errors in tense are excessive.	
Transition	Appropriate transition exists between all paragraphs and within paragraphs.	Appropriate transition exists between most paragraphs and within most paragraphs.	Transition is weak and/or missing between paragraphs or within paragraphs.	
Direct Quotes	All direct quotes are appropriate and complete.	All direct quotes are appropriate, but some are incomplete.	Has inaccurate and/or missing quotes. Quotes cited may be incomplete.	
Grammar and Punctuation	The paper is nearly free of grammar and punctuation errors.	Errors of grammar and punctuation do not fall into patterns and are not excessive.	The paper exhibits patterns of errors in the areas of grammar and/or punctuation.	
Spelling and Vocabulary	The paper is free of spelling and word-choice errors.	Errors in spelling and word choice are minimal and not repetitive. Errors do not inhibit meaning.	The paper exhibits patterns of errors in spelling and word choice. The errors are excessive and/or inhibit meaning.	
APA Format	The paper follows APA style guidelines.	Errors in APA formatting are minimal.	Errors in APA formatting are excessive.	
Total Score				

Scoring: A=32–36; B=28–31; C=25–27; D=23–24; F=Below 23
N/A: not applicable

Figure 4.3

Rubric for Scoring Reflective Journals

Name: _____ Date: _____

Skill	Excellent (3)	Adequate (2)	Unacceptable (1)	Score
Format	Entry is correctly formatted with identification of response, page in text where it can be found, and the response.	N/A	Entry is missing the page number and/or identification of the response.	
Quality of Response Selection	Response selection is relevant and significant to the meaning of the text.	Response selection is relevant but is not significant to the understanding of the text.	Response selection is superficial and does not contribute to the understanding of the text.	
Quality of Response	Response evidences thinking that is literal, analytical, and makes connections between the text and the reader's experiences.	Response attempts to analyze the text but does not attempt to make connections between the text and the reader's experiences.	Response is literal.	
Length of Response	The ideas evidenced are fully developed.	Most of the ideas are fully developed.	Most of the ideas need to be developed with more information.	
Grammar, Punctuation and Word Choice	Entry is written in complete sentences and is nearly free of grammar and punctuation errors. All of the words are used correctly.	Entry is written in complete sentences. Some errors in grammar and punctuation exist, but they do not appear to be in a pattern nor do they inhibit the understanding of the response.	Entry may not be written in complete sentences and/or may have excessive errors in grammar and/or punctuation. Errors in word choice inhibit the understanding of the response.	
Total Score				

Scoring: A=14–15; B=12–13; C=10–11; D=8–9 **Grade:** _____
Note: The total grade will be lowered for journals that are missing assigned entries.

Steps for Designing an Effective Rubric

1. List the learning outcomes of the assignment. Specifically, what do you want your students to know and be able to do? (For example, you may want your students to research and present an oral report on a given topic; use support materials and props; have good eye contact; and use appropriate body language, expression, and volume.)

2. List the formatting criteria that you expect to be followed in the assignment (such as introduction, supportive details, conclusion).

3. List the usage and grammatical criteria that you have for the assignment (e.g., use of complete sentences, spelling, punctuation, correct use of scientific terms).

4. For each criterion, determine what will be regarded as Excellent (3), Adequate (2), and Unacceptable (1). *Note:* There must be *discernible differences* between the expectations of each criterion. Problems arise when the differences are slight. (For example, a clear difference should exist between an excellent and adequate performance.)

5. Convert the scores into grades, following your school's grading policy. (For example, a student who scores 24 out of 27 points in a school that has 90–100 as an *A* would receive an *A* on the assessment.)

Once you have set up your original rubric, you can easily modify it to address the specific criteria for each assignment, which is preferable to using a generic rubric that may not account for what you are assessing.

Note: Always distribute and review scoring rubrics with the students when you give them the assignment to ensure that the performance expectations are clear *before* they begin the assignment. To eliminate confusion and possible misunderstandings, it's a good idea to give students a sample assignment, ask them to score it using the rubric, and discuss their scores in relationship to your own. To help you get started, Figures 4.2 and 4.3 on pages 78–79 provide sample rubrics for you to consider.

Designing Authentic Assessment Tools

Not all students test well for a variety of reasons. Some students have difficulty with the format of objective tests. Some students overthink the test questions and lose sight of what the questions are asking. Some students freeze when faced with a test and literally shut down. For students like these, what they produce during an examination period speaks only to their test behaviors, not to what they know or to what they are capable of doing. To properly and fairly assess these students, teachers need authentic, alternate forms of assessment that allow students to demonstrate their knowledge using a format that is understandable and accessible to them. Authentic assessments closely mirror the kinds of activities that students will experience outside the classroom. They are usually performance based and are often collaborative. Activities such as formal presentations, performances, portfolios, experiments, inventions, movies, computer animations and games, journals, original writings, PowerPoint presentations, research, interviews, exhibitions, surveys, and debates would fall into this category.

Note: While authentic assessments clearly benefit poor test-takers, they are equally beneficial to good test-takers. Authentic assessments give all students opportunities to collaborate, develop, and practice good critical-thinking skills, while at the same time providing opportunities for students to explore ways they can apply what they are learning to the world outside the classroom.

Guidelines for Developing Authentic Assessments

1. Activities should be challenging, meaningful, and tied to instruction.
2. Activities should be clearly defined (what the activity is, what skills or concepts will be demonstrated, time frame, etc.).
3. Activities should be aligned to the student's learning style.
4. Students who are capable should participate in the selection, design, and planning of the activity.
5. Students should be given a rubric prior to the beginning of the activity to identify performance expectations.
6. Student progress should be monitored throughout the activity to ensure that the student's work is on target.

Steps for Designing an Authentic Assessment

Step 1. Clearly define the project. It is important that both the student and the teacher have the same understanding of what the student is being expected to produce. Having a written agreement between the student and the teacher that clearly defines all aspects of the project is a good way to ensure that this happens. The most successful projects are those that are designed and developed collaboratively by the teacher and the student. When defining the project, be sure to include the following information:

- What it will be or what form the project will take (such as presentation, PowerPoint, survey, dramatization, movie, research).

- What skills, concepts, or body of knowledge will be exhibited in the project. These skills and concepts should be aligned with your instruction.
- The scope of the project. For example, if the project is a survey, how many participants will be included; if there is an expectation of research, how many sources will be included.
- How the project will be used to determine the quarter or semester grade.
- The time frame for the project, including when the project is due.
- When the student will work on the activity.
- What materials or equipment will be needed and who will assume the responsibility for getting those resources.
- If students are collaborating, how they will be working together, what responsibilities each will assume, and so on.
- How, when, and to whom the project will be presented.

Step 2. Set up an ongoing assessment schedule. It's important that the student's progress be checked periodically throughout the project to ensure the work is on target. Divide the project into segments and assign each segment a due date when you will meet with the student to assess what has been done to date.

Step 3. Develop criteria for scoring. Rubrics are ideal for scoring authentic assessment because they can be easily customized to accommodate differences in projects. When you meet with students to develop a scoring rubric, bring a list of the specific criterion that you want this project to exhibit.

Step 4. Develop a tool for student evaluations. If the projects are going to be presented to the class, it's a good idea to guide students' responses with specific questions instead of just asking, "What did you think?" When designing a student evaluation form, frame the questions in a way that would give the presenter *positive* feedback. For example, "What did you like most in the presentation?" or "What did you learn?" or "What would you like to know more about?" are more sensitive and more helpful than asking "What would you have done differently?" or "What would make this presentation better?" It's also a good idea to stay away from having students rate each other's performance (poor, good, very good, excellent, etc.). These evaluations typically tend to reflect how the students feel about each other rather than provide useful feedback on the work being presented. See Model 13: Authentic Assessment.

 ## Using Portfolios to Assess Student Learning

A portfolio is an assessment strategy that can be used to measure student growth over time and over projects. The portfolio is a collection of an individual student's work that is systematically collected at regular intervals and exemplifies his or her expertise in a given area. The portfolio can be used to collect and evaluate varied sources of information that demonstrate a student's learning and competence in terms of process (*how* the student reaches a goal) and product (*what* the student produces). Both teachers and students value portfolios as a form of assessment because they allow for a more complete and comprehensive view of a student's abilities and competencies. Unlike some tests, which only show what a student recalls, portfolios provide students with the opportunity to *demonstrate* not only what they know but also what they can do and how well they can apply what they know to other areas of their lives. In addition, portfolios reflect the student's ability to set and achieve learning goals, something that is not readily seen in a single exam.

Guidelines for Developing Portfolios

1. The contents of the portfolio should be challenging, meaningful, and tied to instruction.

2. Teachers and students are partners in the educational process. They work together to assess student strengths and weaknesses, establish learning goals, select products to be included in the portfolio, and evaluate portfolio contents.

3. The contents of the portfolio are clearly defined (learning goals, pieces to be included, how the pieces demonstrate the learning goals, how the portfolio will be assessed, time frame for completion, etc.).

4. Portfolios are multidimensional, taking into account student interests, learning needs, experiences, and goals.

5. Students are required to be reflective and to self-assess.

6. Students are evaluated against themselves, not against other students.

7. Assessment is systematic and ongoing.

8. Samples are collected systematically over time and are used to measure student growth.

Implementing Portfolio Assessments

Keep in mind when developing your portfolio assessment strategy that it is an ongoing decision-making process. Some of the decisions should be made collaboratively with the student or students who will be responsible for the portfolios (contents, goals, assessments, organization, etc.) and some of the decisions should be made in advance of your first collaborative meeting (what learning their portfolio will demonstrate, logistics, due dates, when students will work on their portfolios, etc.).

Because portfolios are unique assessment tools, there are no set rules about what shape a portfolio takes. Some portfolios are housed in folders, some in crates or boxes, and some electronically. Likewise, there are no rules about what goes into the portfolio. They are collections, representative samplings of the student's work. They can be collections of writing, art, musical compositions, artifacts, experiments, and so on. It is important that the student and the teacher have a written description of the project that reflects their common understanding. Some of the decisions you and your students need to consider when implementing portfolio assessments include the following:

- The purpose of the portfolio.

- The kinds and number of learning samples that should be included.

- The skills, concepts, and knowledge that will be demonstrated in the portfolio.

- What the portfolio will assess (types and quantities of errors, thinking and problem-solving strategies, ability to apply skills and concepts, ability to edit, process, final products, etc.).

- The logistics (where the portfolio will be kept, how often students will work on the portfolio assignments, when students will work on their portfolios, due dates, etc.).

- The lessons that need to be taught to support student success with the portfolio assignments.

- How the portfolio will be organized.

- How the portfolio will be assessed.

- When conferences will be held to review portfolio progress.

- How evaluations of the portfolio will be used.

- How students will self-assess.

Portfolios can be multidisciplinary and represent work over the course of an entire year; however, it is not necessary to begin your portfolio assessment agenda on such a grand scale. Until you become comfortable with the process, it's advisable, when first starting out, to limit the scope of the portfolios, with the understanding that they can be expanded with new learning goals and activities once previously set goals have been met. Model 14 is an example of an initial writing portfolio that was limited to five samples. Models 15 and 16 give students the opportunity to reflect on and self-assess the work included in the portfolios. Figure 4.4 provides a rubric for scoring portfolios.

The key to success when using portfolios as assessment tools is organization. Having clearly defined expectations, procedures, and activities will reduce the anxiety and ensure an exciting and productive learning experience for both you and your students.

Figure 4.4

Rubric for Scoring Portfolios (Grade 6)

Name: _____ Date: _____

Assignment: _____

Learning Goals	Topic Paragraph	Supporting Paragraph	Conclusion	Neatness	Organization	Spelling and Word Usage	Total
Sample 1							
Sample 2							
Sample 3							
Sample 4							
Sample 5							

Scoring: 3=Excellent; 2=Cood; 1=Needs Improvement
27–30=A; 24–26=B; 21–23=C; 19–20=D

Topic Paragraph

    3: Well-developed with introductory information that clearly explains what will be discussed in the rest of the paper.

    2: Needs to be developed with more information.

Supporting Paragraphs

    3: Complete with topic sentence, supporting details, and conclusion.

    2: Complete, although some paragraphs need more supporting details.

    1: Incomplete and/or missing supporting details.

Conclusion

    3: Summarizes ideas presented in the paper.

    2: Summarizes most of the ideas presented in the paper.

    1: Missing and/or fails to summarize main ideas.

Neatness

    3: Has margins and is neatly presented.

    2: Has margins but may have marks.

    1: Missing margins and/or is messy.

Organization

    3: Ideas are presented in a logical and an understandable way.

    2: Most ideas are presented in a logical order.

    1: Ideas are not presented in an organized way.

Spelling and Word Usage

    3: All words are used correctly without any spelling errors.

    2: Most words are used correctly. There may be one spelling error.

    1: Errors in spelling and/or word usage make reading and understanding difficult.

Using Assessments to Monitor Student Progress and Inform Instruction

Learning is a lifelong *process* that is continuous and subject to change. Ongoing and student-centered assessments will bring students to this understanding in a very real and personal way. In the past, when assessments were given at the end of a unit, students who failed or did poorly had no opportunity to modify their understanding before teachers moved on to the next unit. Now teachers understand the importance of assessing throughout the unit to identify and address student weaknesses so that students don't fail. These ongoing assessments can take a variety of forms. Anything that gives you information regarding your students' knowledge and understanding can be used as an assessment tool. For example:

- *Homework and class assignments* can help identify student strengths and weaknesses in a particular area. To quickly identify areas that need more instruction, ask students to self-assess assignments by identifying those questions or problems that gave them difficulty and the reasons why or at what point they experienced difficulty. Also ask students to identify problems or tasks they felt were particularly easy.

- *Objective quizzes* given at the beginning of the period help assess reading comprehension quickly and easily. These quizzes need not be long. Five questions (typed) will tell you very quickly if students understand what they read. These questions should be significant to the meaning of the text (How did John react to the news of his friend's death?) as opposed to identification of trivia (What was John wearing when he was told of his friend's death?). *Note:* If a student indicates that he or she is doing the reading but is still performing poorly on the quizzes, refer the student to the reading specialist for an evaluation to see if a reading problem might be preventing the student from understanding.

- *Response journals* help assess student understanding. Ask students to write a reflective response to something in their reading that resonated for them to help you see disconnects in understanding or interpretations that may not surface in class discussions. Through response journals, teachers can sustain the assessment by dialoging with students via written personalized responses to the students' responses.

- *Graphic organizers* help students to organize concepts and data in a visual way. Because the information is typically displayed in words or fragments, they provide a quick and easy way to see if or how students are connecting ideas. (See Chapter 6 for examples.)

- *Teacher observations* help capture information that escapes formal evaluation. Teachers *see* behaviors or responses that could affect or explain student performance (in either a positive or a negative way). These observations, which could be either academic or behavioral, should always be recorded, dated, and used by teachers to inform decisions about a further course of action. (See Model 17: Teacher Observation Form.)

■ *Teacher questioning* is a classic strategy and is used by teachers to assess student knowledge and understanding and their academic strengths and weaknesses. Ask both literal questions (that assess knowledge) and probative questions (that assess comprehension and ability to apply information) during class discussions or informally during casual conversations.

■ *Student-teacher conferences* are an effective way to ascertain information regarding your students' learning. Most students feel more comfortable sharing difficulties with their teachers one on one rather than in a whole-class setting. To maximize conference time, both you and your students should bring a written list of issues you want to discuss. Keep a record of each meeting, documenting the discussion and the decisions made during the meeting. (See Model 18: Conference Report Form.)

■ *Student writings* give teachers a great deal of information that can be used to inform instruction. These writings don't have to be long. A ten-minute writing in response to a prompt prior to beginning a unit or lesson will reveal issues students are having with their writing and organizational skills as well as their knowledge, beliefs, or positions on issues that are integral to the lesson or unit. Mid- and post-teaching writings are also good ways to monitor student progress and learning.

■ *Student self-assessments* help teachers get a more complete picture of student learning, needs, and related issues. Journal entries, learning logs, and self-evaluation forms are typical tools used for this type of assessment. (See Model 19: Self-Evaluation Form and Model 20: Learning Log for Self-Evaluation). Students should self-assess frequently; they need practice being reflective. Many teachers ask students to self-assess at the end of each class period as a strategy for informing their next day's lesson.

■ *Peer reviews* can be seen as a teaching tool as well as an assessment tool. Having students evaluate other students' work reinforces their own knowledge and understanding, while honing skills they can use for their assessment of their own work. *Note:* For peer reviews to be productive, students must be given a rubric to clarify and guide their review of another student's work. The use of a rubric gives the students a sense that their papers are being evaluated fairly. They also provide talking points for students to use to discuss their evaluations with each other and with you following the reviews.

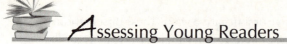
Assessing Young Readers

Reading is the bottom line to all learning. Good readers are advantaged with the vocabulary, skills, and strategies that allow them to access all the content areas; poor readers, regardless of ability, are conversely disadvantaged. They are like tennis players competing in a high-stakes match without a racket. They can't succeed. For this reason, how reading instruction is addressed in the early years is critical to a child's success in school and to the range of possibilities and opportunities that follow.

As a classroom teacher, you have the social, ethical, and professional responsibility to teach *all* the children in your class to be good readers. This can happen with a sound reading program that includes a wide range of assessments that are systematic, are administered frequently, and identify individual strengths and weaknesses. This system of assessments could include, for example, informal reading inventories, running records, anecdotal records, story retelling, and developmental checklists, and writing assessments in addition to interest surveys, reading logs, journals, portfolio assessments, writing samples, teacher questioning, and conferencing. Maintaining an assessment portfolio throughout the year for each student will make it easier to assess each student's performance and progress comprehensively and reliably.

Informal Reading Inventories

It's important that students be given reading materials that are appropriate for them, materials that are challenging but not so difficult that they would frustrate and shut down the reader. Informal reading inventories (Cooter, 1990) help teachers identify the reading level of each student so that appropriate texts can be selected. These assessments, which identify a student's ability in graded or leveled reading materials such as basal readers or books used for guided reading, characterize reading levels as independent (easy to read), instructional (ideal for teaching), or frustration (too difficult). Periodic administration of these inventories helps teachers assess student progress and informs the teacher when the student is ready to be moved to the next level of reading. Among the inventories that are frequently used in schools today are *Classroom Reading Inventory* (Silvaroli, 1986), *Developmental Reading Assessment* (Beaver, 2001), *The Flynt/Cooter Reading Inventory for the Classroom* (Flynt & Cooter, 1998), and *The Flynt/Cooter English*Español Reading Inventory* (Flynt & Cooter, 1999).

Running Records

A running record (Reutzel & Cooter, 2004), which is taken by the teacher as the student is reading, identifies the student's decoding development as well as what the student can do both independently and with teacher support. The teacher sits beside the student while the student reads a 100- to 200-word passage and records what the student does during the reading. A coding system developed by Marie Clay (1972, 1993a, 1993b) is used to identify how the child responds to each word read (for example, reads it correctly, substitutes an actual word with another word, asks for help, recognizes error and self-corrects). This coding system takes about two hours of practice to master. Most teachers find that the time spent learning the codes is negligible compared to the benefits to their students. The results of the assessment tell the teacher with 90 percent reliability if the book the child is reading is appropriate. Giving a child a book that is too difficult frustrates and demoralizes the child, which often translates into the child being turned off to reading. Conversely, giving a child a book that is too easy will quickly bore the child and cause him or her to lose interest in reading. The goal is to help children become independent readers and lovers of books. Giving students books that are challenging, interesting, and manageable is the first step in making that happen.

Running records also help teachers group students effectively for guided reading. By taking frequent running records, the teacher knows when the student is ready to move to another group. A final benefit is that while running records help teachers monitor the progress of their students, they also verify for them the success of their own intervention strategies. Teachers monitor the progress of their students; they also verify the success of their own Intervention Strategies. For procedures for taking, scoring, and analyzing Running Records, see *www.readinga-z.com/guided/runrecord.html* or *www.eworkshop.on.ca/edu/pdf/calculatepercentaccuracy.pdf*.

Anecdotal Records

Anecdotal records (Winograd, Flores-Duanas, & Arrington, 2003) are informal observations made by the teacher as the students are working. These records are helpful in identifying behaviors that do not present themselves on traditional tests and assignments, behaviors that may be impeding student success. For example, Ms. Anderson, while taking anecdotal records during learning-center time, noticed that Alex was having difficulty getting started. By the time he finally began working productively, most of the other children were finished. Had his teacher not been observing Alex, she may have misinterpreted his failure to complete the assignment as inability, disinterest, or inattentiveness when the real problem was his weak organizational skills, something she now knows she has to address.

Although there are no steadfast rules about taking anecdotal records, many teachers find it helpful to select a focus for a particular set of observations (such as organization, comprehension, interactions with other students, time-on-task).

Because these records are informal and individualized, it is not necessary to observe all of the students on the same day. It is necessary, though, that the same behaviors or competencies be observed multiple times during the year so that you can monitor both student progress and the success of your intervention strategies. See Model 21: Anecdotal Record.

Story Retelling

Story retelling can be used to assess students' comprehension and ability for literal recall (Fountas & Pinnell, 1996) and to identify their sense of story structure. This assessment, which usually immediately follows a student's reading of a story, requires that the student retell the entire story in sequence, as the teacher notes the recollections. You may want to look for the following skills and concepts during this assessment:

- the accuracy of the sequencing
- the accuracy of the events being recalled
- evidence of elements of structure (beginning, middle, end)
- accurate identification of major events in the story
- accurate identification of minor events in the story
- accurate portrayal of characters
- references to elements of text (theme, setting, plot, etc.)
- inferences and judgments made by the reader
- recollections of supporting details
- connections readers make between the text and their own lives

Your analysis of the students' retelling will help you identify what areas of instruction need more attention. Like all assessments, to accurately assess student growth, conduct retelling assessments several times during the year. See Model 22: Story Retelling.

Developmental Checklist

A developmental checklist will help you monitor individual or group progress. The best checklists, which are teacher developed and focus on a particular set of skills or behaviors that can be easily observed, are simple to develop and can easily be used to monitor students' progress on a weekly basis. The checklist in Model 23: Developmental Checklist was created to monitor student behaviors before, during, and after reading.

Assessing English Language Learners

As the numbers of limited or non-English-speaking students continue to increase in classrooms throughout the United States, teachers in larger numbers are being faced with the challenge of developing strategies that will enable them to assess these students in ways that will yield high degrees of reliable information that they can use to inform their instruction. What confounds this problem for most teachers is their inability to converse with their students in their native language and their understanding that it is impossible to obtain accurate information about student knowledge if that knowledge is being assessed in a language or a format the students don't understand. To compensate for the disparity in languages, teachers are rethinking how they assess their students and providing alternate forms of assessments and/or modifications to their existing assessments and procedures. These modifications could include the following:

1. Replace traditional testing with authentic, performance-based assessments.

2. State the questions in active rather than passive voice (for example, change "If a man left his family . . ." to "If you left your family . . .").

3. Align materials and texts to students' language proficiency level.

4. Allow students to use a list of terms or vocabulary words with definitions that would help them understand the expectations of the assignment or test.

5. Provide the questions or directions in both the student's native language and English.

6. Give students extra time to complete the tasks.

7. Test students separately to alleviate the discomfort and distraction of taking more time than their English-speaking classmates.

8. Provide students with models of test questions and responses.

9. Simplify the test questions, removing all unnecessary language.

10. Allow students to use bilingual dictionaries.

11. Give assessments that rely on graphic and visual content and verbal responses instead of on dense texts.

12. Allow students to be assessed as part of a collaborative group.

Sharing the Results

Keep the lines of communication open between parents, teachers, and students, particularly when it comes to grades and student performance. While teachers understand that grades are just a small piece of the big picture, parents and students continue to see grades as the most important piece. You can diffuse unnecessary student and parent anxiety about grades by simply being open about your grading procedures and by sharing student progress throughout the year with periodic updates in addition to the report cards. Like rubrics, progress reports objectify grades and make it clear to parents and students *how* the grade was determined.

Progress reports should be specific. For example, reporting that Tom has missed four of the last six assignments has more meaning than "Tom's weakness is homework." A standardized form is best for these updates. They don't take much time to fill out, and they're easy for students and parents to read and understand.

The frequency for sending progress reports is up to the teacher. Many K–5 teachers find sending them weekly is a good strategy for keeping the students on target and for keeping the parents involved in their children's learning. Should you decide to do this, alert parents in advance of the day they should expect their children to bring these reports home. For middle and high school teachers, because of the number of students, it is more realistic to provide these reports at the middle and at the end of each marking period.

The Power of Assessments

Although we would like students to think of assessments in positive terms, as tools that are used by their teachers to make curricular decisions that will in turn lead to their successful learning, the truth of the matter is that most students think of assessments as being punitive. Undeniably, assessments hold a great deal of power for students at all levels of learning, and this power is felt at an early age.

Inadvertently, teachers and parents condition children to view assessments as being negative by the very language and behaviors they use to discuss and respond to assessment results. As early as kindergarten, answers are designated as being either right or wrong, with the *right* answers being rewarded with smiles, smiley faces, and hugs, which, at home, children receive for *good* behavior. As children proceed through school, they come to understand that for them to move forward with their friends, they have to do well on tests and assessments. They understand that not to do well means they will be left back. In addition, for many children, parental approval and consequent social life and privileges are connected to their performance on assessments. A poor report card could easily translate into weeks of staying in on Saturday nights until the grades improve. In high school, the power of tests is felt even more as students come to understand that their ability to get into the college of their choice or to receive scholarship support will be predicated on how well they perform on school-based and standardized tests and assessments.

The probability that you can change this perception is low. However, you can be sensitive to the stress and anxiety that students experience with testing. Understand that students do take test results personally, even if they don't acknowledge it. Understand the ramifications testing can have on students' self-perceptions, and understand that you can make a difference in *your* class by assessing frequently and by working with your students to use those assessments to improve their learning and consequent summative results.

Advice from the Field

- If a significant number of students do poorly on an assessment, check to see if the instrument is flawed before making the assumption that the students didn't study or that they didn't understand the material.

- If an assessment is going to be graded, make sure you give students ample notice so that they can study. It's a good idea to give students at least a week's notice for a major exam.

- Always set your students up for success. Make sure they have the skills in place *before* they are tested.

- Always find something good to say about a student's work or performance.

- Always begin and end assessment conferences with something positive.

- Don't use tests or the threat of tests to control your students. It sends the wrong message about the function of testing.

Additional Resources

Butler, S. M., & McMunn, N. D. (2006). *A teacher's guide to classroom assessment: Understanding and using assessment to improve student learning.* San Francisco: Jossey-Bass, Inc.

Clay, M. M. (1985). *The early detection of reading difficulties* (3rd ed.). Portsmouth, NH: Heinemann.

Clay, M. M. (1997). *Running records for classroom teachers.* Portsmouth, NH: Heinemann.

Harp, B. (1994). *Assessment and evaluation for student-centered learning.* Norwood, MA: Christopher-Gordon.

Stiggins, R. J., Arter, J. A., Chappuis, J., & Chappuis, S. (2007). *Classroom assessment for student learning: Doing it right—using it well.* Upper Saddle River, NJ: Prentice Hall.

References

The AP vertical teams guide for English (2nd ed.). (2002). New York: The College Entrance Examination Board.

Beaver, J. (2001). *Developmental reading assessment*. Parsippany, NJ: Celebrations Press.

Clay, M. M. (1972). *Reading: The pattern of complex behavior*. Exeter, NH: Heinemann.

Clay, M. M. (1993a). *An observation survey of early literacy achievement*. Portsmouth, NH: Heinemann.

Clay, M. M. (1993b). *Reading recovery: A guidebook for teachers in training*. Portsmouth, NH: Heinemann.

Cooter, R. B., Jr. (Ed.). (1990). *The teacher's guide to reading tests*. Scottsdale, AZ: Gorsuch Scarisbrick.

Flynt, E. S., & Cooter, R. B., Jr. (1998). *The Flynt/Cooter reading inventory for the classroom*. Scottsdale, AZ: Gorsuch Scarisbrick.

Flynt, E. S., & Cooter, R. B., Jr. (1999). *The Flynt/Cooter English*Español reading inventory*. Upper Saddle River, NJ: Merrill/Prentice Hall.

Fountas, I. C., & Pinnell, G. S. (1996). *Guided reading: Good first teaching for all children*. Portsmouth, NH: Heinemann.

Gardner, H. (1983). *Frames of mind: The theory of multiple intelligences*. New York: Basic Books.

McWorter, K. T. (2000). *Guide to college reading*. New York: Longman.

Reutzel, R. D., & Cooter, R. B., Jr. (2004). *Teaching children to read: Putting the pieces together* (4th ed.). Upper Saddle River, NJ: Pearson.

Silvaroli, N. J. (1986). *Classroom reading inventory* (5th ed.). Dubuque, IA: William C. Brown.

Stanford, P., & Reeves, S. (March/April 2005). Assessment that drives instruction. *Teaching Exceptional Children, 37*(4), 18–22.

Winograd, P., Flores-Duanas, L., & Arrington, H. (2003). Best practices in literacy assessment. In L. M. Morrow, L. B. Gambrell, & M. Pressley (Eds.), *Best practices in literacy instruction*. New York: Guilford.

Online Resources

Edutopia—www.edutopia.org/assessment
Teacher Vision—www.teachervision.fen.com/assessment/resource/5815.html
Center for Teaching—http://cte.umdnj.edu/student_evaluation/evaluation_cat.cfm
Rubrics for Teachers—www.rubrics4teachers.com

Authentic Assessment: Grade 10 Language Arts

Name: _____ Class: _____

Teacher: _____ Date: _____

Project: Write an original short story, five to eight typewritten pages, about a conflict between two characters that thematically shows man's insensitivity to man. The story will include description and dialogue and will be written in complete sentences that are free of grammar and punctuation errors.

Project Participant(s): John Arlington

Skills/Concepts/Knowledge: The story will demonstrate an understanding of the progression of plot (exposition, rising action, climax, falling action, and conclusion), conflict, theme, paragraph development, grammar, and punctuation.

Scope: N/A

Time Frame: Four weeks; project due 2/22

Work on Project: Work on the project will be done during class on Fridays and at home.

Resources needed: None

Project Review Dates: Teacher-student conferences will be held during class on Mondays and after school by appointment.
> Conference 1: Outline Due—2/1
> Conference 2: First Draft Due—2/8
> Conference 3: Second Draft Due—2/15

Presentation of the Project: The story will be shared with the class during an oral reading on 2/22.

Evaluation of the Project: The project will be evaluated with a rubric developed by John and Mr. Peters.

How the Project Will Be Valued: The story will be 20 percent of the second-quarter grade.

Sandra's Writing Portfolio

Title Page

Letter to the Reader (describing the goals and contents of the portfolio)

Baseline Sample
> Title: My Bedroom
> Assessment of Strengths and Weaknesses

Descriptive
> Title: A Day at the Beach
> Personal Comments (explaining why the piece was selected,
>   what specific goals were being addressed)
> Rough Draft
> Self-Assessment

Expository
> Title: How to Plant a Rose Garden
> Personal Comments
> Rough Draft
> Self-Assessment

Narrative
> Title: The Day My Brother Was Born
> Personal Comments
> Rough Draft
> Self-Assessment

Persuasive
> Title: A Dress Code Is Needed at Selby High School
> Personal Comments
> Rough Draft
> Self-Assessment

My Best Piece
> Title: Shopping with My Grandmother
> Personal Comments
> Rough Draft
> Self-Assessment

Portfolio Reflective Self-Assessment

Name: _____ Date: _____

Title: _____

1. My goals for this piece were _____
   _____.

2. The goals I met were _____
   _____.

3. The goals I did not meet are _____
   _____.

4. What gave me the most difficulty on this piece was _____
   _____.

5. What I did to solve the problems I was having was _____
   _____.

6. What I would do differently on the next piece is _____
   _____.

7. What I like most about this piece is _____
   _____.

8. What I have learned is _____
   _____.

9. What I would like to know is _____
   _____.

10. What I need help with is _____
    _____.

Portfolio Final Self-Assessment

1. What goals did you set for your portfolio?

2. What goals did you meet?

3. What goals did you not meet?

4. What problems did you have while working on your portfolio?

5. How did you solve each problem?

6. What did you find easy while working on your portfolio?

7. What did you enjoy most about working on your portfolio?

8. What would you do differently the next time?

9. How could your teacher be more helpful to you?

10. What are your goals for your next project?

Teacher Observation Form

Teacher: _____ Class: _____

Date	Student's Name	Observation	Action

Conference Report Form

Date: _____ Conference Site: _____

Conference Participants: _____
_____
_____

What Was Discussed:
_____
_____
_____
_____
_____

Decisions Made:
_____
_____
_____
_____

Conference Follow-up:

What Student(s) Will Do:
_____
_____
_____

What Teacher Will Do:
_____
_____
_____

What Parent Will Do:
_____
_____
_____

Date for Follow-up Conference: _____

Self-Evaluation Form

Name: _____ Class: _____

Date: _____ Lesson: _____

What I learned today:

What I thought was most interesting:

What I thought was least interesting:

What I found confusing:

What I would like to know more about:

Learning Log for Self-Evaluation

LEARNING LOG			
Name: _____ **Class:** _____			
Date	What I Learned	What I Don't Understand	What I Want to Know More About

Anecdotal Record

Teacher:					
Student:					

Guided Reading	Writing Workshop	Learning Center	Independent Work Time	Free Time	Action Needed

Comments:

Story Retelling

Sequence of events in the story	Supporting details
1. _____	1. _____
2. _____	2. _____
3. _____	3. _____
4. _____	4. _____
5. _____	5. _____

Recollections of characters (physical, behavioral, attitudinal)

_____

_____

_____

Identification of conflicts

1. _____

2. _____

3. _____

4. _____

5. _____

Setting

_____

_____

References to literary devices (theme, tone, plot, etc.)

_____

_____

Inferences/judgments

_____

_____

Connections made between text and student's personal experiences

_____

_____

Teacher's observations/comments:

Student strengths:

Student weaknesses:

Developmental Checklist

Group: _____ Date: _____

Text: _____

Behavior	Sally	Tom	Andy	Pam	Sara
Before Reading					
Begins immediately					
Makes predictions based on title and cover					
Shows enthusiasm for reading					
Asks questions about the text					
During Reading					
Uses visual information to support comprehension					
Questions during reading					
Makes predictions					
Self-corrects					
Rereads to confirm accuracy and/or understanding					
After Reading					
Draws conclusions					
Makes personal connections with story					
Connects story elements with other stories					
Asks questions					

Comments:

5

Literacy Instruction K–12

A variety of methods and materials may be used to teach literacy K–12. Highly effective teachers must teach students to read with comprehension and fluency, to write using the writing process, to listen effectively, and to speak comfortably and correctly. Studies have shown that it is neither the materials nor the methodology but rather the teacher that makes the difference in literacy instruction (Paterson, Henry, O'Quinn, Ceprano, & Blue, 2003). Arguably, some materials and methods are better than others, but believing in your purposes and your goals and knowing the important basic components of an excellent literacy program will guide you in your teaching of literacy.

This chapter begins with a discussion of balanced literacy because it has implications for all readers and writers. It includes the essential components of literacy that may be adapted for all levels of instruction. Although teachers often associate balanced literacy with elementary students, its components and tenets can easily be incorporated into all lessons in middle and high school as well.

Secondary teachers can benefit from a deeper understanding of how students learn to read. Many middle and high school students are unprepared to read grade-level content material. This may be extremely frustrating to teachers who expect that the students will understand the text and their lectures. Students with learning disabilities, reading issues, and/or English Language Learners (ELLs) have needs that must be addressed by middle and high school teachers. Most traditionally prepared teachers who have had many education courses have a difficult time teaching their content to all students; for alternate route teachers, it presents a more difficult challenge. We believe that providing a framework such as balanced literacy, which explains a successful way to teach literacy, will benefit teachers of all grade and content levels.

Balanced literacy represents what scholars in the literacy field have learned over the past fifty years, which is that literacy instruction must consist of a balance or combination of various approaches to be effective and to meet the needs of students. Much has been written about phonics or skills-based instruction versus whole language or a more holistic approach that focuses on the use of great literature. That debate has raged for years, but it is now understood that both of these approaches have great merit and should be incorporated into all literacy instructional programs. Students need a variety of approaches that can provide a well-rounded approach to learning. Different types of learners need different approaches and balanced literacy offers a variety of instructional modes, which is a key to its success.

What Is Balanced Literacy?

Balanced literacy is a literature-based framework for teaching literacy behaviors, attitudes, and skills to children. It is a comprehensive approach to teaching students how to read, write, speak, think, and view. The ultimate goal of balanced literacy instruction is to foster a love of reading and writing that will inspire and challenge students to develop as lifelong learners who naturally think of themselves as readers, writers, speakers, and thinkers. This is accomplished by using authentic reading and writing experiences to teach students how to use literacy strategies and skills and by giving them many opportunities to apply what they have learned. This process is used at all levels of instruction.

Advocates of balanced literacy instruction (Cooper & Kiger, 2003; Mazzoni & Gambrell, 2003) believe that for students to develop as good readers, writers, speakers, thinkers, and viewers, the teaching strategy must include the following:

- Literacy must be the foundation of all lessons. In content areas, focusing on how to read the text is as important as mastering the content.

- Strategies and skills must be taught directly and indirectly, in small and large groups, as well as in individualized settings.

- Reading instruction must include word recognition, phonics, comprehension, fluency, vocabulary instruction, small-group instruction, large-group instruction, and independent work.

- Writing instruction must include an understanding of the *process* of writing, which students can apply to all types of pieces (such as narrative, expository, descriptive, poetry, journal writing, letter writing, etc.) as well as instruction in grammar, punctuation, and spelling.

- Reading and writing opportunities must extend into all content areas (math, art, music, social studies, science, etc.).

- The same strategies used to teach reading and writing should be applied in the same way to teach the content areas.

What Are the Components of a Balanced Literacy Program?

To maximize effectiveness, a balanced literacy program should include all areas of literacy presented in context, informed by assessment, and designed to meet the needs of all students, as outlined on page 109 and discussed later in this chapter.

What We Want Our Students to Know and Be Able to Do

Teachers at all levels of K–12 instruction must plan lessons with a clear understanding of exactly what they want their students to know and be able to do by the end of the lesson. School and district curriculum guides, based on state and

Strategies Teachers Can Use to Guide Students' Reading

Major Components	Strategy	Targeted Skills
Read-Aloud	Interactive reading in which students listen to the teacher reading, often joining in on familiar refrains or repetitious words.	Story conventions, comprehension, fluency, word sounds, function of punctuation, vocabulary, phonics.
Shared Reading	Together, students and teacher read aloud from a text (big book, enlarged text, poem, song, or part of a story, etc.).	Story conventions, vocabulary, fluency, word sounds, function of punctuation, phonics.
Reader's Workshop	Students self-select book to read. Teacher presents minilesson to target skill/concept for students to locate in their book during their independent reading, which follows the minilesson.	Targeted skills or concepts specific to the workshop.
Independent Reading	Students read self-selected texts alone or with partners.	Reading strategies, vocabulary development, reading appreciation, concept development.
Word Work	Teacher directly teaches letter knowledge, phonological awareness, high-frequency words, letter and word sounds and patterns.	Word-attack strategies, vocabulary, phonics, grammar, letter knowledge, letter/word sound connections.
Guided Reading	Teachers work with small groups as they read leveled texts that match student abilities and interests. The teacher helps students think, read, and talk about the text in a purposeful way that will lead them to become independent, strategic, fluent readers.	Word-attack strategies, story conventions, fluency, comprehension, vocabulary, phonics.
Write-Aloud	Teachers model what they are actually thinking as they write a piece in front of their students.	Writing conventions, concept development, writing process.
Shared/Modeled Writing	Teacher and students work together to compose messages and stories. Students provide the ideas as the teacher acts as scribe, modeling the writing process.	Writing conventions, concept development, syntax, vocabulary development, grammar, writing process.

(Continued)

continued

Major Components	Strategy	Targeted Skills
Interactive Writing	Teacher and students compose a story or message together. Students "share the pen" to record the text on the board, poster, or overhead.	Concept development, writing conventions, sounds of words and how sounds connect with letters, writing process, punctuation, grammar.
Guided Writing	Teacher works one-on-one or in small groups with students, focusing on specific skill deficiencies.	Sound/symbol connection, process writing, writing conventions, punctuation, syntax.
Independent Writing	Students self-select topics, draft, edit, revise, and either publish or record their writing in personal journals.	Writing conventions, process writing.
Writer's Workshop	All students in the class work independently on self-selected pieces at the same time.	Writing conventions, process writing.
Literacy Centers	Places for students to practice and explore skills and concepts while guided reading groups are in session.	Reinforce skills and concepts taught in class.

Ancillary Components		
Student-Teacher Conferences	Teacher meets one-on-one with students to discuss skill and concept strengths and weaknesses.	Targeted skills and concepts are specific to the needs of the individual student.
Direct Instruction	Teacher presents planned skill or concept instruction to whole class or small groups.	Targeted skills or concepts are specific to the lesson (i.e., vocabulary, phonics, writing conventions).
Literature Circles	Students meet in small groups to discuss, question, and challenge other opinions about text.	Analytical thinking and speaking skills, comprehension, discussion skills.
Minilessons	Small-group or whole-class instruction on a specific skill or set of skills with which the targeted group is having difficulty.	Targeted skill or concept is specific to the lesson.
Thematic Units	Teacher plans and presents literature-based units of instruction that include opportunities for students to read, write, speak, present, respond, and think critically.	Comprehension, connecting ideas, story and writing conventions, word-attack skills.

Major Components	Strategy	Targeted Skills
Field Trips	Class trips are planned to support student learning.	Add to student understanding and knowledge base. Help students make connections between what they are learning and life outside the classroom.
Guest Speakers	Guests (parents, teachers, administrators, support staff, community members, etc.) support student learning with personal experiences.	Add to student understanding and knowledge base. Help students make connections.
Guest Readers	Guests read favorite stories to the class.	Literature appreciation, listening skills.

national standards, typically identify the specific teaching and learning expectations for each grade. Certain basic teaching and learning goals should be part of all balanced literacy programs. For example, we want our students to know

- the conventions of print (Freeman, 2003)
- strategies for approaching text
- a wide range of vocabulary words
- strategies for decoding words
- conventions of grammar and how they are used to communicate meaning
- the process of writing
- how to speak effectively and how to organize an oral presentation

In addition, we want our students to be able to

- read with fluency and understanding
- use context clues to understand text
- make predictions and draw conclusions from information presented in texts
- express their thoughts verbally and in writing in a clear and logical way
- edit their work
- be reflective and ask questions

- be academic risk-takers
- participate meaningfully in class discussions and activities
- work collaboratively and independently and be able to monitor and pace themselves
- apply what they learn to other areas of their lives

 ## Using the Balanced Literacy Approach to Teach Students to Read

Using a balanced literacy approach to teach students to read involves using a model of gradually reducing the amount of support we give to students. We begin by giving them extensive support by modeling and sharing new tasks, gradually lessening the amount of support we offer when we provide guided practice and then independent practice. Our goal is to help students become independent readers.

Learning to read and write is similar to learning any new skill. Consider how a child learns to ride a bicycle. At first, a child must see how a bike is ridden. This action is usually *modeled* by a parent who demonstrates how to ride a bike. Obviously, the child must know where the hands and feet are placed. After the modeling, the child *interacts* with the parent in a *practice setting* where the child has the opportunity to ride the bicycle with a parent holding it. The next step is *guided practice,* in which the child rides the bicycle and the parent runs alongside, helping if necessary and offering just the right amount of support. Ultimately, of course, the goal is for the parent to let go and for the child to ride *independently*. This teaching model works for all levels of instruction with all types of activities.

Read-Alouds at All Levels of Instruction

Learning to read can be done using a similar strategy. Begin by reading aloud to your students to model for them what the reading process looks like and sounds like and to provide them with a background knowledge about texts that will help them in their later efforts. Read-alouds are important for students in preschool through high school. Specifically, reading aloud

- actively engages students with the text
- introduces them to the fluency of a good reader
- teaches students how to read

- gives students the opportunity to hear the cadence of the language

- supports students' critical-thinking skills

- engages students' meaning-making processes throughout the reading

- fosters students' understanding that it is their responsibility to create meaning

- fosters a love of reading

Ways to Do a Read-Aloud

A read-aloud can be structured in several ways. It may be used to teach strategies and skills or it may be used simply to foster a love for reading. Read-alouds are critical for young children as well as for middle and high school students.

Step 1. Before Reading
a. Create enthusiasm for the text.
b. Introduce the students to the author and the illustrator.
c. Discuss the title and ask for predictions relating to the title.
d. Discuss the illustrations on the cover.

Step 2. During Reading
a. Ask questions that will activate prior knowledge.
b. Ask students to predict what they think will happen next.

Step 3. Reading Aloud
a. Read to students in an expressive, exciting way.
b. Read through the whole book for young children, a chapter or a piece of text for older students. Allow them to hear the fluency in your reading.

Step 4. After Reading
a. Ask questions about the characters.
b. Discuss the elements of the story (characters, plot, problem, solution).
c. Create a graphic organizer or chart to categorize the information for the students.
d. For young children, you may reread the story several times. Students love to hear stories over and over again.
e. For repetitive text or stories or poems with a refrain, ask students to read or sing along with you.
f. Ask students what they think would have been a better ending for the story.
g. Encourage students to make personal connections to the text.

Step 5. Providing Suggestions for Follow-up Activities (which may also be used as independent activities)
a. Read another book on the same topic.

b. Create a piece of artwork relating to the text in some way.
c. Search a magazine for ideas or objects discussed in the book.
d. Research a topic presented in the book.
e. Write a journal entry responding to the text.
f. Write a response or letter to the character.
g. Write a sequel to the story.

If you decide to do a read-aloud simply for the students' listening pleasure, provide a simple introduction to the book and let the students relax and begin to understand the joy of books and the value of listening.

Reading aloud models fluent reading, familiarizes students with language and conventions of books, and exposes students to different genres of literature. It also introduces vocabulary, and provides motivation to students by exposing them to topics they may otherwise not be ready to read on their own.

Shared Reading

Shared reading is another strategy for students to use to practice their reading skills. Whether in a small group or with the entire class, this is a time when students share in the process by reading along with you. This offers students the opportunity to hear fluency and expression in your reading and to hear you talk about the strategies you are using *while* you are reading. With younger students, you may want to use big books and have students join in by reading familiar words, refrains, or repeated text. For older students, you may bring in a piece of nonfiction or a text that offers a different perspective on a topic that you are studying. For example, teaching the Holocaust strictly from a textbook may not offer personal accounts of human suffering that may be found in a personal memoir or trade book that can be shared with the class. Shared reading also gives teachers the opportunity to challenge students by reading books that are too difficult for students to read on their own, but ones they can still understand and enjoy as they follow along, reading silently. This offers them a shared-reading experience while giving them an opportunity to activate their prior knowledge or to learn new information.

Reading Workshop

Because independent reading is always the ultimate goal, teachers must provide students with many opportunities to read independently. Reading workshop is an excellent strategy to use to foster a love of reading and to encourage students to participate in self-selecting books that they are interested in reading. Prior to the independent portion of the reading workshop, teachers present a five- to ten-minute minilesson, targeting a specific skill or strategy. These strategies can come from the scope and sequence of a basal reading series or a district curriculum guide or from students' work. During the minilesson, the teacher explains the skill or strategy, models what students are to do, provides examples, and conducts a think-aloud. Following the minilesson, students are directed to read independently and look for the strategy in their reading. For example, if you teach a minilesson on describing words (adjectives), you would discuss what an adjective is, provide some examples of interesting adjectives on the board or on an overhead, and read a short piece from a text that has wonderful adjectives. You then provide the students with sticky notes and ask them to look for adjectives in the book they're reading and to place sticky notes on some "excellent adjectives" that they recognize as they read. Students enjoy this activity and it provides a focus in their reading. It doesn't interfere with their reading, and it helps to keep them on track. Teachers often follow up this activity by asking students to respond to their reading in their journals or reading logs. After about 20 to 30 minutes of reading (depending on the grade level), the class gets together for a group share, at which time students are invited to share their favorite adjectives.

Minilessons may be conducted on all sorts of topics, including how to find the plot, setting, parts of speech, elements of good writing, adverbs, lead sentences, and so on. Teachers often use the independent reading portion of reading workshop to walk around the room, conferencing with students either for a few seconds or a few minutes, depending on the teacher's purpose. Reading workshop provides a purpose for reading and an opportunity for all students, including struggling readers, to participate meaningfully as valued members of a community of readers. Reading workshop for middle and high school students offers the opportunity to read a self-selected book that is on their level. The book may be read at home or after other work in the classroom has been completed.

Independent Reading

Independent reading, sometimes referred to as SSR (sustained silent reading), allows students to choose the books they want to read (Fountas & Pinnell, 2001). Students can select books from the classroom or school library, or they can bring books or magazines from home. Independent reading not only gives students private time to practice their reading skills but also sends students an important message that reading is not just an activity associated with "schoolwork." We want students to know that reading is enjoyable and valuable. Giving them time to read something that is of high interest to them quickly sends that message.

In some classrooms, independent reading is a time for unmonitored reading, a time when students self-select their texts and are not responsible for doing an activity relating to their reading. This can present a challenge for some teachers because some students spend their time changing books, flipping through books, or pretending they are reading. Independent reading can be most beneficial when teachers hold students accountable for their reading. That may mean that after the independent reading, the teacher takes three to five minutes to have students either meet with a partner or in a small group and tell each other a few interesting ideas about their book or to have students respond to their book in a journal or meet with the teacher in a conference to talk about the book.

Word Work

Word work, an important part of a balanced literacy program, should be included in every day's activities (Bear, Invernizzi, Templeton, & Johnston, 2003). It begins with a brief, focused experience intended to expand students' language and literacy skills. Although instruction varies based on the grade and ability level of the students, word work includes a variety of language and word activities:

- *Phonics and phonemic awareness strategies* are particularly important for children in grades K–2, who use these strategies to figure out how to pronounce and understand words.

- *Word wall* is a place where teachers post new words or frequently used words for the students to learn and practice. The words on the word wall are changed often and are practiced every day. They may be chanted with younger students or just repeated with older students.

- *Interactive edit* is used to teach mechanics, spelling, or grammar. Students work with the teacher to make corrections together. This is a great activity for middle and high school students because they are doing authentic work with their peers' writing.

- *Journal writing* gives students the opportunity to use their words in a fun and creative way. Journals may or may not be read by the teacher. Some teachers like to give their students a place to privately express their feelings. When pages are private, students fold over the page and the teacher agrees not to read that page.

A word wall may be used at all levels of instruction to reinforce vocabulary instruction.

- *Creating morning messages* is a way of working with language and words in a meaningful context. Teachers write messages on the board and students respond.

- *Vocabulary words* in a paragraph are featured and discussed either in groups or with the whole class. They should be introduced in context, in phrases or in sentences, to help students understand and be able to actually use the new words.

Note: Word work must not consist of isolated activities; rather, it should be done in context, using authentic text. Using a great piece of literature to teach letter sounds, verbs, or expressive language is the best way to teach a word lesson because it allows your students to associate their learning with something that makes sense to them.

Guided Reading

Guided reading provides students the opportunity to read and practice the strategies that good readers use, such as rereading when they don't understand or using context clues, while benefiting from the teacher's guidance (Fountas & Pinnell, 2006). The goal of guided reading is to train students to become strategic readers who use the strategies they learn to decode words and make meaning of what they are reading. Guided-reading instruction is usually done in small groups of four to six students and includes the following steps:

1. *Introduction:* The teacher introduces the book using a variety of strategies (providing background information, asking students to recall a previous book or author, asking students to make predictions based on the cover, etc.).

2. *Book Walk:* The teacher conducts a book walk with the students by going through the pictures in the book and asking students to make predictions about what they think is going to happen, what they think the book is about, and so on.

3. *Reading:* Younger students will "whisper read" while one student reads aloud in a slightly louder voice. More fluent readers read the book silently. Teachers can periodically check on an individual's reading by asking the student to read a portion of the text aloud.

4. *Discussion:* A discussion following the reading gives students an opportunity to discuss their understanding of the text and to explain how they used their "target" strategies to reach that understanding.

Note: The ultimate goal of guided reading is to have the students become silent, independent readers reading connected texts—readers who, just like you, call on the strategies that good readers use to understand what they are reading. Although guided reading has traditionally been a teaching activity for elementary students, the steps have implications for all levels of instruction. The basic format is simple. The teacher introduces the book, targeting a strategy that may help students; the students read the book and then discuss it, including how they used the target strategy.

For guided reading to be effective, students must be placed in flexible groups where they are reading on their own instructional level. If students are reading texts that are too difficult, students will become frustrated and they will give up. Placing students in appropriate groups prevents that from happening. The groupings are strategically formed by using assessment results (running records or individual reading inventories) and teacher observations. As students develop as readers, they advance to groups that are reading more difficult texts. To ensure that students are moved into groups as soon as they are ready, teachers should take a running record on one student individually after each guided-reading session. Taking a running record is a relatively simple and expedient way to ensure that all students are placed appropriately. (For more information on running records, see Chapter 4, pages 98–100.) In addition to grouping students appropriately, teachers must select texts that match the students' reading level. Most book publishers identify the instructional level of their texts. You can also go online to identify books and their levels. You may check the following websites to access information about books and their levels:

BSD: Leveled Books Database at www.beavton.k12.or.us/home/staff/library/books/leveling

Hoagies' Gifted Education Page at www.hoagiesgifted.org/reading_levels.htm

Leveled Book Lists at www.home.comcast.net/~ngiansante/

Muttnomah County Library School Corps: Reading Levels for Books at www.muttcolib.org/schoolcorps/readinglevels.html

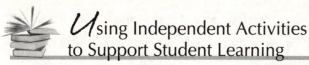

Using Independent Activities to Support Student Learning

Whenever teachers think about organizing the classroom for guided reading, the question of what the other students will be doing while the teacher is with one small group always surfaces. This is a good question; it takes a strong plan to make this work. Students need to learn to be independent learners, responsible for completing tasks and for managing their own time. To teach these crucial skills, students work on independent activities while the teacher is working with guided-reading groups.

Independent activities may be organized in a variety of ways. For younger students, literacy centers, typically organized around the perimeter of the room, are where students go to practice the skills and concepts taught during class. The centers change frequently to accommodate the skills and concepts that need to be reinforced with practice. Independent activities may be organized so that each student in the class has several activities that must be completed within a certain time period. A Group Work Board organizes students into small groups in which each group has specific activities they must complete as individuals. Following are examples of activities you may want to include in your classroom:

- *word center,* where students can practice putting words together to make sentences or practice spelling new words

- *reading center,* where students can reread books that were read during read-alouds or shared readings or can read additional books on topics discussed in class

- *art center,* where students can create pictures to illustrate their understanding of a story read in class or to illustrate their own stories

- *listening center,* where students can listen to books on tape, while following along with the book

- *writing center,* where students can practice writing their letters or create original pieces of writing

- *math center,* where students can practice their math skills

- *science center,* where students can make observations and take notes on what they see (for example, plants growing, an ant farm, an aquarium)

- *music center,* where students can work together to write their own song about the plot or a character in a story

- *recording center,* where students can tape-record their reading of a book

- *computer center,* where students can do research or practice skills with educational games and tutorial programs

- *drama center,* where students can write and perform plays or skits

Note: Independent activities do not consist of busywork. The activities must be meaningful and authentic with real purposes. Each activity must be strategically planned with goals, objectives, specific directions, materials, and so on. Students should be required to produce something tangible in each center (e.g., a piece of artwork, a review of the book, a tape recording, a checklist). Having to produce a product at each center helps students focus and direct their time. It also gives them a clear message that this is their "work" and that what they are doing is important.

Using a Group Work Board is a highly recommended way to organize students' responsibilities and to differentiate instruction. A Group Work Board is a structure that includes all the students' names written on sticky notes in groups of five or six. Under each sticky note is a series of activities that students should be working on during independent-activities time. (See Figure 5.1.) These activities should be completed by the end of the week. Depending on the teacher's purposes, these groups can be self-selected or created by the teacher. They are typically not the same groups as the guided-reading groups. Sometimes, students are randomly grouped; other times, students who need to be working on similar assignments are grouped together. Although the types of activities vary from week to week, the Work Board always includes independent reading. Some teachers use icons for the Group Work Board to identify for students where they should go or what they should do during literacy-center time. For example, icons may be used to designate a location (e.g., the computer center, math center, writing center, reading center) or an activity or assignment (e.g., research a topic, practice a play, read independently).

During independent activities, students choose their activity, work at their own pace, and manage their own time in order to complete the assigned work by the end of the week. For independent activities to work effectively, students need to understand that they are expected to work quietly and independently, without interrupting the teacher while the teacher is working with guided-reading groups. Some teachers use a "Do Not Disturb" sign, while others wear a specific hat or necklace that signifies guided-reading group in progress. Students must respect the fact that teachers cannot be interrupted. Should students have a question or a problem, they are told to "Ask three before me." They may ask three classmates if they have a question, but if they do not get an acceptable answer to their question, they must wait until the teacher is available. Students can always choose another activity from the Group Work Board or read independently.

Figure 5.1

Group Work Board

Mrs. Gray's Classroom
Group Work Board
For Independent Activities

Jessica Jared Robyn Michael Harry	Judy Richie Alana Jeremy Josh	Kitty Al Sam Jake Mo	Jane Howard Jill Jennifer Royce	Matt Michele Peter Hannah Marvin
Reading Journal	Listening Center	Independent Reading	Partner Reading	Literature Circle
Computer	Literature Circle	Word Work	Poetry	Computer
Independent Reading	Poetry	Read Around the Room	Reading Journal	Independent Reading
Word Work	Independent Reading	Computer	Browsing Box	Word Work
Poetry	Readers Theatre	Overhead Projector	Independent Reading	Partner Reading

Use sticky notes for groupings of students. Change groups frequently.
Put reattachable tape on the back of the activity card so that you can change activities each week.

This process does not happen without effort, however. Teachers must model activities from the Group Work Board and provide opportunities for students to work while the teacher walks around the room checking on student assignments and answering questions. Using the first four to six weeks of the school year to model independent activities every day will ensure that students understand their responsibilities, learn how to work independently using the Group Work Board, and accept that this is a time when their teacher cannot be interrupted. As soon as independent activities run smoothly (usually by the beginning of October), the teacher may begin guided-reading groups.

Using the Balanced Literacy Approach to Teach Children to Write Write-Alouds

Because reading and writing are so closely related, you will find that many of the reading components of balanced literacy are aligned with the writing components. The goal in both reading and writing is to construct meaning. Students in elementary, middle, and high school write using similar strategies. During write-aloud, teachers model what they are actually thinking as they write a piece in front of their students. This should be done on the board or on a flipchart so that the students can follow along as the teacher composes. As they write, teachers express concern over word choices, asking the students to help revise and edit their work. Teachers may discuss why they began the piece with a particular opening and ask for suggestions for revision. This component is extremely helpful to students because it shows them the process writers have to go through to get to their finished product. It also helps students understand that writing is not easy and that it takes time, thought, and revision, even for the teacher.

Shared Writing

Shared writing requires that the teacher and the students take part in the writing process together (Freeman, 2005). They choose a topic together and decide how it will be written. In addition, they consider the voice, the audience, the form, and the purpose of the piece. During shared writing, the students provide the ideas, while the teacher acts as a scribe, modeling the process of putting the ideas into written language on the board, on a flipchart, or on an overhead projector. This strategy works with all levels of writers because it provides an opportunity for students to practice thinking and writing like a writer while having the support and guidance of the teacher.

Interactive Writing

Interactive writing is a fun activity in which the students and the teacher compose a story or message together and then "share the pen" to record the story or message on the board, a flipchart, or an overhead. The teacher uses this time to focus instruction on the conventions of writing, word sounds, cadence, spelling, and vocabulary (Fountas & Pinnell, 2006).

Guided Writing

Guided writing allows teachers to provide guided practice as they write their own pieces (Freeman, 2005). This strategy is often used by teachers when working one-on-one with students to help clarify the writing process as they are engaged in the actual process and to address individual problems as they present themselves. This strategy is also used as a whole-class activity. For whole-class guided writing, the teacher divides the class into small groups of students who share similar problems with their writing. As students meet in their groups to discuss aspects of their writing or writer's craft, teachers are free to move about the room and conference with them in small groups. This is particularly successful when students have similar needs at the same time. It allows teachers to focus on the needed skills and strategies without including students who do not have the same needs. An additional benefit of guided-writing groups is that they are short-term groupings, which prevents students from using the groups to identify themselves or their classmates as poor or struggling writers. This is another strategy that can be used for elementary, middle, and high school students.

Independent Writing

Like independent reading, independent writing is a major focus of the balanced literacy program. There are many ways to structure independent writing; however, all of them involve using the writing process, which consists of a series of stages that ask students to think as writers think and to write as writers write. Students need to understand that writers do not just sit down and write a piece without planning, drafting, revising, and editing. Having students engage in writing as process helps to bring them to this understanding in a very pragmatic and meaningful way. The writing process involves five stages: prewriting, creating the first draft, revising, editing, and publishing.

Stage 1: Prewriting   All writing, regardless of the genre, requires a prewriting stage when students strategically choose topics, consider their purpose for writing, identify their audience, select the form the piece should take, determine the information they would like to express, and decide on an organizational pattern for their piece. This stage, which is often omitted by students, is a critical piece of the writing process.

Students can approach this stage in the writing process in various ways. For some students, creating an outline works best; for others, a list seems more appropriate; and for still others, a web or graphic organizer is most useful. For students in the last group, many types of graphic organizers are available that can help them organize their thoughts during the prewriting stage. Teachers should introduce students to all of these strategies and then let students decide which works best for them.

Stage 2: Creating the First Draft   Once the prewriting stage has been completed, the student is ready to write a first draft. This drafting stage is the time for students to write without concern for spelling, punctuation, or other mechanics, knowing that this is the first draft and that this writing will be revised and edited several times before the piece is finished. Instruct the students to skip every other line so that there is room for added words and sentences, arrows, cross-outs, and other revisions. This is important because this is what "real" writers do—they revise and edit—and you want to encourage your students to be authentic thinkers and writers.

Stage 3: Revising   During the revising stage, students refine their ideas and make changes to their work to make their pieces more interesting and more complete and to reflect their purposes in a more meaningful way. Revision is often accomplished with the help of others, either a writing buddy or a writing group, who offer constructive suggestions for revisions. It is important when students share their writing during the revising stage in an author's chair (a special, decorated chair) or in a small group, that students be taught acceptable ways to comment on their classmate's writing. During this stage, appropriate comments must be modeled frequently by the teacher so that students understand exactly how to comment sensitively and effectively. A strategy for students to use to guide their comments is "P.Q.S.: Praise, Questions, and Suggestions." This strategy requires that students begin by finding something about the writing that they can compliment, even if it is as simple as "I like the topic you chose" or "I liked your opening" or "I liked your use of interesting details." Then students must think of questions related to their classmate's writing. For example, if the piece is about a dog, the student might want to know more about the dog (e.g., its name, age, or breed). Finally, students must make suggestions to improve the piece, perhaps adding more details or changing the opening, for example. Making this a procedure that all students must follow lessens the probability that students will find the criticisms hurtful. An added bonus of this strategy is that it teaches students very important life skills: (1) how to make appropriate comments, (2) how to find the good in people, (3) how to be sensitive to other people's feelings, and (4) how to help others.

Stage 4: Editing   Students should understand that revising is all about the content, and editing is all about the mechanics and the final form. Editing consists of checking for punctuation, capitalization, spelling, usage, sentence structure, and form. Students should first edit their own work. Then they should submit it for your review. Your review should identify errors, not correct the errors. Begin by putting a dot at the end of a sentence where there is an error so students can find it, identify it, and fix it. If they cannot find the error, they should come back to you for additional help. At this time, you assist them by limiting their search by putting a dot on top of the incorrect word or phrase so that they can go back and make the correction. If they cannot correct their own errors, show them the corrections and then consider a series of minilessons on editing. While this process may take a great deal of time at first, it is most important that you include it in your practice. Students will never learn to edit unless they have continued practice editing their own work.

Stage 5: Publishing   Publishing is the opportunity to present students' writing to an audience of classmates, parents, or the community. There is a tremendous feeling of pride at this stage of the writing process, regardless of the age or grade level of the students. One way for students to publish their work is to take their writing and make books that they can share with the class. Sometimes, the books are simple, stapled booklets; other times, the books are a bit more fancy and are made of cardboard and covered with wallpaper or cloth. Often, students illustrate their stories with personal drawings or pictures from magazines. Regardless, an important part of this process is to share writing with members of the class. Using an author's chair, students can read their published writings to the class. After reading, students may take turns asking questions and complimenting the author's writing. To ensure that students are treated sensitively, make sure that students are taught how to act appropriately before you begin this activity.

Writer's Workshop

Using the concept of writing as a process is also the way to approach writer's workshop. Writer's workshop, like reader's workshop, begins with a minilesson, includes independent reading and writing, and ends with a group share. Writer's workshop provides students with opportunities for authentic reading and writing. In writer's workshop, students have writing folders for their works in progress. In addition, they keep writing notebooks for jotting down ideas, thoughts, and future writing topics as ideas come to them. The teacher begins with a minilesson, focused on a strategy or skill in writing; and students are asked to consider that particular strategy as they proceed in their writing. These minilessons most often come from weaknesses noted in students' writing.

During writer's workshop, teachers may circulate through the room, conference with students, and offer assistance when needed. Students work at their own pace as they go through the stages of the writing process individually. Because students may be at different stages of their writing at any given time, teachers should do a status check at the beginning of each writer's workshop to see where everyone in the class is in terms of the stages of the writing process.

During the last ten to fifteen minutes of writer's workshop, students gather to share their pieces in the author's chair. This is a time for celebration and praise for the authors. The beauty of writer's workshop is that it allows students in elementary, middle, and high school to write at their own pace in a comfortable environment and to enjoy the applause for their creations, just as real writers do.

Literacy Activities in the Classroom

A program rich in literacy should have a wide range of activities that support student learning. In addition to the major components, a variety of activities should be incorporated into your program to add clarity and interest to your teaching. These activities might include the following:

- *Student-teacher conferences* at all grade levels should be held frequently to help you stay connected to your students as learners and as individuals. These conferences do not always have to be scheduled, nor do they have to be long. Conferencing can easily happen while the class is involved in small-group or individual activities. It is important that students have individual access to your time and attention, especially those students who have difficulty speaking in class and those who have difficulty identifying or verbalizing their problems.

- *Direct instruction* is an effective strategy to teach basic skills and concepts. However, for students to understand these skills and concepts, they must be given opportunities to apply them, practice them, and see them being modeled by their teacher. For example, in a high school history class, teaching students to outline a chapter may be an important skill. However, the process of writing an outline first needs to be modeled by the teacher, showing students how to determine the important details and information, and then practiced by the students. The teacher may provide a partially completed outline and then lead the students to completing it on their own. This will help students to understand the content material better as well.

- *Literature circles* (Daniels, 2002) are opportunities for students to meet in small groups to discuss a piece of literature. These circles are usually no larger than five or six students so that everyone has an opportunity to talk, ask questions, and challenge each other's opinions. For these groups to be effective, students need instruction on how to talk about literature. In the beginning, give groups roles to help them get started. For example, one student may be the discussion leader while another may serve as the group's great vocabulary leader. There can be a group artist or a student in charge of making connections to the text. In elementary classrooms, these roles help to focus students and provide an easier way to maintain a grand conversation. However, in middle and high school, students are better able to function in a group with limited roles. A facilitator is important to keep students on task. The teacher's role is simply to move around the room as the groups are meeting to lend them support, if needed.

- *Minilessons* are great for addressing issues as they present themselves. For example, if you see that students are having difficulty understanding how to use commas appropriately, stopping the class for a quick minilesson on commas, while they are having the problem, will have more meaning for students than waiting and learning comma usage out of context. In a high school science classroom, a minilesson on the differences between vertebrates and nonvertebrates using a semantic map may help students better understand the lesson on the animal kingdom.

- *Critic's Corner* provides students with the opportunity to view films and to think about and talk about what they are viewing in a critical way. For this to be effective, students need to be given the conventions of film and initial guidance about the kinds of things they should be looking for while watching a film. As always, students should be encouraged to make connections between what they are viewing and other areas of their academic and personal lives.

- *Thematic units* provide students the opportunity to explore a specific topic over a period of time (generally one to two weeks), using a variety of activities, texts, and tools. Organizing difficult concepts in thematic units helps students understand those concepts and issues by giving them multiple opportunities to explore them in a variety of different ways.

- *Field trips* help students see how what they are learning is applied in real-life situations. They also help students build a knowledge base that students can call on to help them understand what they are reading. For example, for students who have never seen a live animal, visiting a zoo or farm makes stories about animals come to life.

- *Guest speakers,* like field trips, help students make connections between what they are learning in class and the world outside of the classroom.

- *Guest readers* are fun and inspirational to young readers. Having a parent, the principal, a nurse, a custodian, the librarian, a crossing guard, another teacher, a police officer, a firefighter, or the mayor come in and read their favorite story quickly sends the message that reading is something that is a part of everyone's life and, more important, something that should be an integral part of their lives as well.

- *Oral presentations* are wonderful ways for students to practice their organizational and presentation skills. These presentations need not be long and can be about anything—sharing of personal experiences or possessions, book talks, projects, plans, and so on. Students must have a clear understanding in advance of the expectations of the presentation. For example, you may require students to have a beginning, a middle with three descriptive or supportive ideas, and an ending to their presentations.

These activities provide students with a variety of interesting formats that can be used to teach the skills necessary for literacy development. Teaching with a repertoire of strategies offers students opportunities to learn content while improving literacy with motivating, thoughtful activities.

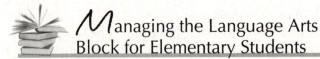

Managing the Language Arts Block for Elementary Students

A balanced literacy program provides a wide range of activities for teachers to use to teach and develop literacy skills. In many elementary schools, literacy is delivered in 90-minute daily blocks of time. Because there are too many activities to fit into a single 90-minute slot, it becomes necessary for teachers to develop weekly agendas that are comprehensive yet varied. When developing their teaching agendas, teachers should select the activities that best support the goals and objectives of the lessons with the understanding that all of the activities should be a part of their overall academic program. Because the program is intended to be flexible enough to accommodate the specific needs of the students at a given time, there is no one correct model. When making activity selections, keep in mind that students must be given opportunities to read and write every day. See Figure 5.2 for a sample 90-minute language arts block.

This 90-minute model can easily be modified to accommodate your teaching needs and teaching style. For example, you may choose to do guided reading four

Figure 5.2

Language Arts Block (90-Minute Block)				
Monday	**Tuesday**	**Wednesday**	**Thursday**	**Friday**
Shared Reading (15 minutes)	Read-Aloud (15 minutes)	Shared Reading (15 minutes)	Read-Aloud (15 minutes)	Read-Aloud (15 minutes)
Guided Reading and Independent Activities (50 minutes)	Guided Reading and Independent Activities (50 minutes)	Guided Reading and Independent Activities (50 minutes)	Guided Reading and Independent Activities (50 minutes)	Guided Reading and Independent Activities (50 minutes)
Reading or Writing Workshop (25 minutes)	Reading or Writing Workshop (25 minutes)	Word Work (25 minutes)	Reading or Writing Workshop (25 minutes)	Word Work (25 minutes)

days a week and reserve one day for literature circles or another activity. Strategies such as independent reading, independent writing, and word work can easily be incorporated into independent activities. You need to be creative and strategic in your thinking and planning.

Many elementary schools have a separate, designated writing period. During that time, writer's workshop should be an ongoing process. Teachers who have the luxury of a separate writing period should set aside one day a week for writing as a test-taking genre to familiarize students with the type of writing that is required for student success on standardized tests (e.g., writing in response to a written or an oral prompt, poem, picture, graph, or chart). This is also true for middle and high school teachers. Teachers may focus their students' writing by scheduling minilessons on different writing genres (narrative, expository, descriptive) or by asking students to write in those genres during a scheduled writer's workshop.

The schedule in Figures 5.2 does not show time for a basal reading series, which many districts are using as part of their total elementary literacy program. Basal readers are comprehensive, commercial reading programs that have been around for many years. One problem with using basal readers exclusively is that they are written for a specific reading level, which is most often equated with a grade level and works for the students reading at that particular level. However, many students read either below or above grade level. The question then is how do you use the stories in the anthologies provided with each basal reading series and still have a balanced literacy program? Although they may seem at first incongruous, with a little creativity, you can blend the two programs. First, take a running record or reading inventory to determine the students' instructional reading level. When you know each child's reading level, you can make decisions about how to best teach students who are on different levels, using the basal materials. You might use the stories with small groups of students whose instructional level matches the stories and provide alternate leveled books for the rest of the students until all of the students' reading levels are in line with the basal readers. You might use the stories in the anthology as whole-group activities to expand students' background knowledge, to improve listening skills, and to provide a common text to teach literacy skills and strategies. This will require that you give added support to students whose reading is below the level of the text. You will also need to supplement the reading of students who are reading above the level of the basal text. If you do not do so, they will quickly become bored or distracted—behaviors that can easily turn into discipline problems if not addressed. Keep in mind that students need a wide variety of reading and writing experiences in their literacy program. To give your students a more appropriate, balanced program, basal programs can easily be supplemented with balanced literacy strategies (such as read-alouds, write-alouds, shared reading, guided reading, reader's workshop, writer's workshop, independent reading and writing, word work, literacy centers, etc.).

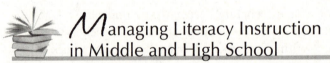

Managing Literacy Instruction in Middle and High School

Because teachers are often faced with 40-minute periods in middle and high school, it can be more challenging to manage literacy instruction for students. Teachers recognize that older students need literacy instruction as much as elementary students. Although elementary teachers are charged with teaching literacy, middle and high school teachers also must teach literacy; for some students, high school is their last chance to learn to read and write well enough to function in the world. For other students, it is a chance to build on what they learned in elementary school. For the more successful students, it is a chance to perfect and practice their skills in order to be prepared for the rigors of college.

The section on literacy activities highlights learning situations that are adaptable for all levels of instruction. High school teachers must begin to think in terms of literacy development. Generally, the expertise in a particular content area is what guides and informs secondary instruction. However, learning to read a textbook efficiently and learning to write clearly in the content area will help students in all areas. After all, doesn't all of the material you ask students to study in your classes utilize literacy skills? For example, there are many ways that teachers naturally incorporate literacy into a secondary classroom. Math teachers ask their students to explain in a journal exactly how they came up with their answers. Chemistry teachers use lab reports as a way to help students incorporate science vocabulary into their writing. American history teachers teach students how to read their textbook most efficiently. They teach outlining skills, note-taking systems and the use of graphic organizers to provide students with the skills that will help their proficiency in the content class while improving their overall literacy skills. Literacy is part of almost everything we do; we must keep highlighting it to students so that they can see the relationship between what they are learning and how they are learning.

There are a number of instructional strategies that secondary teachers can use to help students see how to best understand those relationships, including working with challenging text, comprehending text and learning to study for tests. Although this chapter focuses on ways of introducing literacy strategies to students, the next chapter addresses many more strategies to use in your specific content area.

Research supports the use of instructional strategies to promote literacy learning and reading in content-area classrooms (Greenleaf, Schlenbach, Cziko, & Mueller, 2001). By teaching students how to study, how to read the textbook, and how to study for tests, teachers are providing a tremendous advantage that will stay with students forever. One question that comes up frequently is why secondary teachers need to teach students "how" to read since they are in high school. Shouldn't they already know "how" to read? Of course they should; however, many secondary students don't know how to read strategically and would greatly benefit from the use of instructional strategies.

The key to teaching strategies lies in the development of a framework for teaching students. The teacher must model all of the strategies and provide adequate practice in order for students to truly understand and use the strategies in a productive way.

Instructional strategies should first be presented to the whole class in the form of a think-aloud. The teacher explains the value of the strategy, how she uses it in her reading of difficult or unfamiliar text, and then walks the students through the procedures. It is best to use content classroom material in the explanation to the whole class in order to elicit discussion from students to help them to better understand the process. From there, small-group work can offer students the opportunity to practice the strategy, support each other, and add to each others' learning. The teacher can walk around the room, making sure that all students understand the processes and are able to soon work independently. Ultimately, all students work independently to implement the strategies learned.

Just as the balanced literacy model suggests, in any appropriate learning environment, we begin with modeling, interactive work with a large group, guided practice and then individual practice, while always working toward independent learning. Although we consider this to be an elementary process, it clearly is the optimum way that people learn, regardless of their ages.

Independent learning always involves students thinking about their own learning, being aware of what they have to do, and then addressing their own needs. Teaching students instructional strategies helps to give students the tools they need to monitor their own learning.

The following are examples of instructional strategies that can provide support and benefits to secondary learners:

- *Think–Pair–Share:* The teacher poses a question to the students and provides time for the students to "think" about possible answers. Next, the student pairs with another student to discuss their thinking. Finally, students share their responses with a larger group or the whole class. This strategy teaches students the value of "thinking" about the reading and learning to collaborate with others. This may sound quite basic; however, most students do not really "think" while reading.

- *Discussion Journals:* After a reading and a discussion, students will be asked to write within the following categories:

  ___ An idea or two that they found interesting

  ___ Two things they would like to know more about

  ___ An idea they want to write about in their journal

  This strategy helps to organize students' thoughts and ideas while reading since they will be told what they will have to do before they begin the reading. It also helps them to "think" while reading.

- *Sorting:* Students generate words or short phrases based on a chapter and write them on index cards. Working individually, they sort their cards into categories and then "think" about the words or phrases and how and why they are important to remember. As a group activity, students meet with others in a group and discuss the words and phrases they chose. This activity gives students the opportunity to select important information from the chapter, think about it, and then discuss their choices with others.

- *Chunk and Jot:* Content material is often dense and difficult so we teach students to read for ten minutes and then stop for two minutes, think about what they have just read, and jot down a note or two or write in the margins of the book (if they can). This helps them to process the information and recognize when they may have to reread or stop to think or look something up in the dictionary.

- *Error Analysis:* Allow students to go back to their tests and analyze their errors to get back one-half of the credit. The must first identify the error, write the correct answer and where it was found, analyze why the incorrect answer was originally written, and then write a sentence or two about how this mistake can be prevented in the future. The beauty of this strategy is in the thinking that a student has to do in order to complete this task appropriately.

- *Charting Content Information:* Based upon a particular topic, have students as a group create key questions along the top of the chart. Under each question, students write what they already know about that question. As they progress with charting, students can list the sources that helped them answer the questions. They also consider if there is further research needed to provide more information about the answers to the questions. The last part of the chart is where students summarize the information they have learned about the questions. The chart looks something like this:

Topic: The Civil War	What were the major causes of the Civil War?	What was the abolitionist movement?	What were some of the major battles of the Civil War?	How did the election of Abraham Lincoln affect the war?	Interesting Facts & Details
What We Already Know					
Data Source					
Data Source					
Data Source					
Further Research Needed					
Summary					

In general, you can help your students create study skills and strategies that will serve them well in their thinking and learning by:

- Making real world connections to what they are learning.
- Breaking complex tasks into simpler parts.
- Modeling thinking aloud.
- Modeling note-taking with lectures and textbook reading.
- Presenting important information in the form of graphic organizers. Encourage students to create their own in order to organize information.

- Presenting vocabulary words in context so that students can have a way of associating words in order to remember them.

- Offering a variety of ways to outline text so that students can find the way that works for them.

- Teaching time management skills by creating schedules for students. Encourage them to create their own after they see the sample.

- Teaching them to monitor their own comprehension and provide them with information on how you comprehend difficult material. Offer opportunities for students to try your methods to see if they are compatible.

Advice from the Field

- Give students daily opportunities to read and write independently.

- Give students time to read connected text at their instructional level.

- Teach students a wide range of literacy skills that will empower them as readers and writers.

- Provide multiple forms of assessments so that students can express their learning in ways that fit their learning styles and abilities.

- Create a chart containing all of the literacy components you need to include in your literacy program to make scheduling easier.

- Be prepared to model all of the activities that you want students to do. Sometimes modeling takes a long time, but it is always worth doing. It helps students understand how to complete a task.

- Be sensitive in your approach to students who have difficulty learning to read or to read well. Treat all students with respect and understanding. Problems in reading have a significant impact on a student's life.

Differentiating Instruction for English Language Learners

For ELLs, teachers must consider the types of activities that will provide the greatest benefit. Although some may need to be adapted, many of the activities you assign and teach to your English-speaking students can be acceptable for ELLs. For example, shared reading works well because it doesn't place the entire responsibility of reading on the English learner; rather, it gives the ELL an opportunity to hear language modeled and still participate in the process.

The language experience approach also works very well in a group or as an individual activity. In a group, ELLs benefit from listening to others create a story and may be able to participate; as an individual activity, the teacher helps the student verbalize what he or she can in order to write a piece in English. The teacher is the scribe and the student retains a copy of the piece to use as practice reading.

Oral language activities such as discussions, debates, conversations, and literature circles expose ELLs to language and encourage them to become involved in whatever way they can. Other ways to help oral language fluency is to use readers theater, role-playing, skits, and rehearsed readings.

Teach literacy to ELLs in the same way that you would teach it to any student who is not functioning on grade level. Modify assignments to make them understandable and to make it possible for students to find success. Differentiating instruction must be done for all students, not only ELLs. When a student's needs are not being met by the general instruction in the classroom, further action must be taken. That action should allow the student to find success.

Additional Resources

Calkins, L. M. (1983). *Lessons from a child: On the teaching and learning of writing.* Portsmouth, NH: Heinemann.

Goodman, K. S. (1996). *Reading strategies: Focus on comprehension.* Katonah, NY: Richard C. Owen.

Morrow, L. M. (2002). *Organizing and managing the language arts block: A professional development guide.* New York: Guilford.

Strickland, D. S. (1998). *Teaching phonics today: A primer for educators.* Newark, DE: International Reading Association.

Online Resources

Vocabulary.com— www.vocabulary.com/wordcity.html

Annenberg Learner— www.learner.org/workshops/readingk2/support/Sound WritingProgram.1.pdf

Essay Punch— www.essaypunch.com

Paragraph Punch— www.paragraphpunch.com

Story-It— www.storyit.com

Kids' Space— www.kids-space.org

References

Applegate, M. D., Quinn, K. B., & Applegate, A. J. (2006). Profiles in comprehension. *The Reading Teacher, 60*, 48–57.

Bear, D., Invernizzi, M., Templeton, S., & Johnston, F. (2003). *Words their way.* New York: Prentice Hall.

Blachowicz, C. L., & Fisher, P. (2004). Vocabulary lessons. *Educational Leadership, 61*(6), 66–69.

Caulkins, L. (2006). *A guide to the writing workshop.* Portsmouth, NH: Heinemann.

Cooper, J. D., & Kiger, N. D. (2003). *Literacy: Helping children construct meaning.* New York: Houghton Mifflin.

Daniels, H. (2002). *Literature circles: Voice and choice in book clubs and reading groups.* Portland, ME: Stenhouse.

Fountas, I. C., & Pinnell, G. S. (2006). *Teaching for comprehending and fluency.* Portsmouth, NH: Heinemann.

Fountas, I. C., & Pinnell, G. S. (2001). *Guiding readers and writers (grades 3–6): Teaching comprehension, genre, and content literacy.* Portsmouth, NH: Heinemann.

Freeman, M. S. (2003). *Building a writing community: A practical guide.* Gainesville, FL: Maupin House.

Freeman, M. S. (2005). *Models for teaching writing-craft target skills.* Gainesville, FL: Maupin House.

Greenleaf, C. L., Schlenbach, R., Cziko, C., & Mueller, F. L. (2001). Apprenticing adolescent readers to academic literacy. *Harvard Educational Review, 71*(1), 79–127.

Mazzoni, S. A., & Gambrell, L. B. (2003). Principles of best practice: Finding the common ground. In L. Morrow, L. B. Gambrell, & M. Pressley (Eds.), *Best practices in literacy instruction.* New York: Guilford.

National Institute of Child Health and Human Development. (2000). *Report of the National Reading Panel: An evidence-based assessment of the scientific research literature on reading and its implications for reading instruction* (NIH Publication No. 00-4769). Washington, DC: U.S. Government Printing Office.

Paterson, W. A., Henry, J. J., O'Quinn, K., Ceprano, M. A., & Blue, E. V. (2003). Investigating the effectiveness of an integrated learning system on early emergent readers. *Reading Research Quarterly, 38*, 172–177.

Pinnell, G. S. (2006). Every child a reader. What one teacher can do. *The Reading Teacher, 60,* 8–83.

Routman, R. (2003). *Reading essentials: The specifics you need to teach reading well.* Portsmouth, NH: Heinemann.

Slavin, R. E., Cheung, A., Groff, C., & Lake, C. (2008). Effective reading programs for middle and high schools: A best-evidence synthesis. *Review of Education Research, 57*, 293–336.

Literacy across the Curriculum

Teachers are often asked how it is possible that students can get to high school with inadequate literacy skills. Year after year, we teach students and many get to high school without the skills necessary to read high school textbooks. What happens to these students? Why haven't they mastered the art of reading in elementary school?

We know that young children are generally excited about the prospect of learning to read and write. They love to be read to. They understand most stories, fairy tales, and nursery rhymes. The elements of the stories are usually clear. Each story has a beginning, a middle, and an end. Each story has characters, a plot, and a solution.

Every elementary teacher stresses the importance of introducing books into the classroom and can attest to the level of interest that students have about reading and writing. At this level, reading is enjoyable and books are available in all genres: mystery, fairy tales, funny stories, adventures, tall tales, and so on.

What happens in fourth grade that dampens the children's enthusiasm for reading? Reading becomes a serious matter. Students are no longer reading just for fun; they are now expected to read informational text from textbooks for content. Students go from reading fairy tales to reading about the American Revolution, and it's a difficult transition partly because of students' lack of exposure to expository writing. Traditionally, elementary teachers have focused on reading narrative pieces and the omission of expository text has left students with inadequate practice in reading and understanding informational text. Recently, authors have been writing more informational, illustrated trade books geared to young children, which has helped to ease the transition to serious reading.

There are other, more complex reasons why students have difficulty with reading. In some classrooms, students are not given the opportunity to read at their instructional level. Many students experience frustration because of developmental difficulties, reading disabilities, or motivational issues. One of the simplest situations to correct, however, is the transition to informational text.

This transition is difficult for both students and teachers. Many teachers do not recognize that different techniques must be implemented when teaching early childhood reading and upper elementary school reading. Teachers must use different strategies when instructing students to read content material. Content literacy, as it is sometimes referred to, addresses the question of how to teach students to read informational text, including textbooks, encyclopedias, content websites, newspapers, magazines, and journals. Content literacy is teaching students how to read informational text, comprehend it, think about it, and write about it.

Experts in the field of literacy are unanimous in their belief that authentic reading and writing prepares students to take on the challenges of content literacy. This authentic reading and writing must begin in early elementary grades.

What Elementary Teachers Can Do to Support Content Literacy

Elementary teachers have a responsibility to prepare students for success beyond their own classrooms. Knowing that students have difficulty transitioning into the content areas, teachers should incorporate strategies, such as the following, into their curriculum, which will help make the transition easier.

- Include content area (e.g., math, science, social studies) assignments and activities in learning centers and independent activities.

- Have students read nonfiction pieces from an early age and provide reading guides to help direct their reading.

- Include stories about content area subjects in the student's assigned reading and writing.

- Have content area books available in the classroom library.

- Introduce students to content area skills (e.g., reading headlines, skimming, note-taking, summarizing, sequencing, distinguishing between facts and opinions, identifying cause and effect).

- Provide students with opportunities to read a variety of texts and have students identify the authors' purposes in writing.

- Require students to defend their opinions about characters, characters' actions, and events in the story with specific examples from the story.

Keep in mind that students, to be successful, need concept and skill teaching and support *before and after* they enter the content area classes. Content area teachers must recognize the importance of literacy in their classrooms and must work to ensure that the skills and concepts students need to have in place to understand complex texts are introduced early and reinforced often with interesting, grade-appropriate materials.

Content Literacy in Middle and High School

Teachers must teach students ways of handling situations when they come across unfamiliar words or concepts in content material. We look to the strategies that good readers use—the strategies that teachers use when they don't understand a text. For example, they use context clues to try to figure out the meaning of the word, or they reread the piece that doesn't make sense. They may continue on in their reading to see if the word is explained later, or they may use a dictionary or put a sticky note on the word and check it later. These strategies must be passed along to the students.

All content area learning is grounded in reading and writing. Regardless of the subject, students have to be able to read, comprehend, interpret, and relate information with a high degree of accuracy to be successful. It is virtually impossible, for example, for students in math and science classes to solve problems and do experiments without reading a text to garner information and without reading instructions to guide their work. When students come to the content areas trained to read and write effectively, content area teachers capitalize on the training these students have had and use the reading and writing strategies the students already have in place. Content area teachers should do the following:

- Teach vocabulary in context instead of from disconnected lists.
- Provide students with multiple texts in addition to the textbook (e.g., magazines, Internet searches, short stories, videos, interviews, newspaper articles).
- Model difficult skills.
- Teach the skills needed to read and understand textbooks.
- Give students opportunities to meet in small groups to discuss, question, and challenge each other's opinions.
- Provide students with reading guides to focus their reading.
- Make sure all student writing is done using the writing process.
- Read aloud to students so that they can hear the language. (This is particularly helpful for students who have limited experience reading textbooks.)
- Think aloud for students so that they can hear what and how they should be thinking about a problem or process.
- Conference with students frequently to ensure they understand the material.
- Require students to keep journals (even in math and science classes). Student entries will help you identify how and what students are thinking so that misconceptions can be addressed before they become problems.
- Assess student progress frequently using multiple forms of assessment.
- Do guided and shared readings and writings with students, particularly at the beginning of the class to help them navigate and understand difficult texts.
- *Always* help students make connections between what they are learning and their own personal lives.

Challenges in Content Literacy

Content material can sometimes present challenges to students. The following suggestions will help teachers work with content text:

- Although textbooks are a source of content information, many other sources are available. Newspapers, magazines, trade books, and videos are just a few examples of ways to provide content information to students.

- Content learning involves all areas of language arts and literacy, not just reading. Use writing, thinking, speaking, and viewing to help students understand and learn content.

- Learn the prior knowledge and experiences of your students so that you can create lesson plans that will meet their needs.

- Expose students to and have them practice using many different types of informational text, such as trade books in various content areas.

- Provide experiences that will help students become strategic readers. Use a model of gradually released support so that you are scaffolding, or providing support to, students until they are ready to work independently.

- Model the strategies that you use as a good reader and help students to develop those strategies using authentic informational text.

- Teachers of all levels and content areas must understand that all teachers teach reading. A chemistry teacher or a history teacher has to teach content using some kind of reading text or material. Help students to learn to read that information more carefully so that you can help the student understand the content more effectively.

- Use thematic units to teach content material because the topics can easily integrate literacy skills and content areas.

- Provide students with direct instruction on how to navigate the text.

Some teachers of content areas ask, "Why do we have to think about teaching reading? The elementary teachers already taught students to read and, besides, we are physics teachers!" Although there is some truth in that statement, elementary school is not the end of the line for the reading train. Students' reading techniques are further refined and they become better as they learn and practice new strategies. Some students do not fully learn to read efficiently until they are older and others have had language barriers that prevented them from reading English well. For these reasons, many students come to a high school class unable to independently read the text. Although some teachers may advocate failing students who don't have the necessary skills, the more compassionate method is to teach these students strategies that will help them grow into better content readers. As teachers, we are responsible for teaching the students who are in our classes.

*E*lements of a Strong Lesson

If we approach content area literacy in the same way that we approach planning any lesson, we begin with a look at the prior knowledge our students bring to the lesson. If we are working on a social studies lesson with a textbook section on the Vietnam War, we must know if our students have any background knowledge that will help them to understand the text. The first element in any good lesson is always *prior knowledge.* We consider what we can do to stimulate a greater understanding of the background of our content area. In some cases, it may simply be a discussion that will bring the time line to the forefront of the students' minds. Or there may be the need for a film to explain the time period to provide a frame of reference. Or the teacher may bring in newspaper articles or magazines to build enthusiasm and interest in the subject. These prelesson activities would yield a very different discussion and level of understanding than the more traditional approach of "Open your book to page 200 and we will read about the Vietnam War."

The next element in building a strong lesson is *purpose setting* for the reading of the text. Setting a purpose helps the reader stay focused while reading and gives him or her something to look for while reading. For example, if I ask you to read a paragraph and then ask you why Mr. Smith went to the store, you may or may not have that answer. However, if I ask you to read a paragraph with a purpose and that is to know why Mr. Smith went to the store, chances are quite good that you will know that answer after you finish the paragraph. Setting purposes for reading a text can sometimes be done by using the subheadings and turning them into questions.

Next, we consider what happens while the student is reading. As the student reads, is he or she looking for important information; looking at charts, graphs, or maps; thinking about what he or she knows; or thinking about what is going to happen? Make students aware of their thought processes while they are reading so that they can self-question, monitor their understanding as they go along, and summarize what they have read. This is called *strategic reading* and it is the cornerstone of building comprehension in content area material. Strategic reading consists of strategies that teachers can model for their students. Teachers must model proper reading strategies for their students in order for the students to learn.

After teacher modeling, students should do a *guided practice.* Remember that the student is attempting each strategy with your guidance and you must provide feedback to help the student achieve his or her goals. At the end of the lesson, the student is asked to summarize what he or she has learned and reflect on the circumstances under which the student might use this strategy again. The follow-up activity is an *independent practice* with a student using the strategy in an authentic situation.

The use of a content area textbook has traditionally been the main tool for learning. Although this has been the time-honored technique, there are problems associated with this way of teaching. First, textbooks are often quite unappealing to students. They are also often too difficult for students to read and understand (Wade & Moje, 2001). Although they have improved considerably in recent years, a book written on a ninth-grade level is still distributed to students who are reading on the ninth-grade level but also given to students in the same class who are reading on sixth-, seventh-, and eighth-grade levels as well. This places tremendous pressure on the teacher, who often winds up reading the book to the class. This is not a great way to teach because students need the opportunity to practice reading and comprehending text. Students need to read materials that they are able to read. There may be magazines, newspapers, and trade books on topics that would be on a more appropriate level for students. These sources would provide the background knowledge students need to maximize their reading comprehension. They can also get a more in-depth view of the topic with outside sources because textbooks often give a cursory look at various subjects of importance.

How students read the content is the next part of designing a strong content lesson. If the textbook is too difficult for your students, you have several options, including reading aloud, reading silently, doing rehearsed readings for oral readings, dramatic readings (rehearsed), partner reading, independent reading, and small-group reading. If you read the text to the students, your purpose will be to provide background information on the topic. That is fine as long as you understand that your students will require other material to read. Students need opportunities to read content materials to develop the skills necessary to understand dense material and informational text. Therefore, you must find other content material suitable for your students' level of instruction. It's important to do what works for your students. Content reading is followed by discussion, activities, projects, group work, and so on. In general, literacy strategies can be used as a guide to help your students maximize their reading ability.

Literacy Strategies

The purpose of using literacy strategies is to provide help and guided practice to students. Often, teachers unknowingly assign work that students have not been shown how to do. Think about note-taking. How many people have actually been taught how to take notes? Did a teacher at one point assume you knew how to do it and say, "Take notes on this chapter"? When you teach note-taking, provide students with a few different systems so that they can choose the one that works best for them. For example, the Cornell System of Note-taking suggests that students divide their paper into two columns, one two-thirds of the page, called *Notes,* and the other one-third column of the page called *Highlights.* Students learn to determine important details in the Notes section and cues to learning in the Highlights section. They practice using a text and then compare their note-taking systems to see what works for them. Instruction that offers an explanation, modeling, and guided practice helps students learn how to be independent learners. Literacy strategies reinforce appropriate skills and understanding.

Study Guides

In addition to using a variety of sources for reading in content areas, the strategies taught to students will help them to become better readers and, in turn, help them to better understand the various content areas. For example, using a study guide is an effective strategy to help students set purposes as they read and helps to direct students through the reading of informational text. Struggling readers would benefit from a study guide that helped them construct meaning because the study guide would be designed to follow the flow of the chapter and provide hints along the way. For a struggling reader, the first study guide given could be modeled by the teacher. The teacher would go over each area, fill in the study guide, and talk about how she or he was able to complete the study guide by reading the content. The study guide provides opportunities for students to reflect, preview, predict, and write their thoughts. As students progress, less and less information would be provided by the teacher with the hope that the student could eventually create his or her own study guide. Many variations of study guides exist; some are questions and sentence completions that follow the chapter's order, others provide hints for studying for tests and for categorizing information.

K-W-L Plus

K-W-L Plus is another strategy that is effective in teaching content material (Ogle, Klemp, & McBride, 2007). This strategy works so well because the process contains all of the elements of a good lesson (What I **K**now, What I **W**ant to Know, What I Have **L**earned). To activate prior knowledge, the teacher asks the students what they know about a particular topic. The students respond and the teacher records all of the statements on the board or on an overhead under the column labeled *K*. When all of those comments have been noted, the teacher asks the students what they want to know or expect to learn about the topic. The teacher records their questions under the column labeled *W*. The students are then asked to read a selection or the teacher reads the selection to the class or the students may watch a film or listen to a tape. After the literacy experience, ask students what they have learned and then record their comments in the *L* column. At this point, the students can discuss their understanding prior to the reading and compare that to what they learned. Were their questions answered in the text, or do they now need to go one step further and find information? Ask students to use that information to write a short

Figure 6.1

K-W-L Chart

Eskimos		
K **What we know**	*W* **What we want to know**	*L* **What we learned**
Eskimos eat fish. They live in igloos. They hunt for food. They live in Alaska. They live in modern homes.	What do they eat? What kinds of schools do they go to? What do they do for fun? How do they like the cold weather? How do they protect themselves from the cold?	They live in houses. They go to schools like we do. They dress very warmly. They eat all kinds of food. Their families are like ours.

Summary paragraph of what you learned:
I learned that Eskimos are just like we are. This was surprising to me because I thought that they were always in big parkas, eating fish, and hunting. I found that they eat similar foods, live in modern homes, and do the same kinds of things that we do for fun. It is much colder in their climate, but they learn to dress warmly.

paragraph about what they learned. Some teachers use this strategy as a way of helping students gather information from a text as a prereading activity to activate schema and set a purpose for reading, others as a way of confirming predictions or as a graphic organizer. Figure 6.1 shows a sample K-W-L Plus activity for the book *Eskimo Boy: Life in an Inupiac Eskimo Village* by R. Kendall (New York: Scholastic Books, 1992).

Today's Class …

A recap of the class is often what students need to help them recall information in the forefront of their minds. Today's Class … is a strategy that offers students the opportunity to take a few minutes at the end of each class to reflect on what they learned. This strategy teaches students the value of reflection and the importance of thinking about the topic and what they learned. Model 24: Today's Class provides an example of the questions a student would reflect on at the end of the class period.

Graphic Organizers

Graphic organizers help students categorize information in a clear, concise way. Because most people respond and remember information that is categorized, graphic organizers provide an excellent format for helping students to recall main ideas and concepts in a text. Visual examples can help students recall and understand information from a text. Model 25: Graphic Organizer is a sample of a simple graphic organizer that can be used in a social studies class.

Story Map

A story map may be used in K–12 to illustrate the common elements of a story. As with all strategies, before you ask students to complete this activity, model the story map so that students know what is expected. A story map can help students organize ideas because students have to think about each of the elements of a story and record them. A story map is a very helpful study aid for a test. Model 26 is a sample story map for a middle school language arts/literacy class.

The G.R.E.A.T. Club

The G.R.E.A.T. Club strategy, which fosters learning in a social context, has worked well in classrooms at many different levels. The G.R.E.A.T. Club, which stands for Groups Reading, Evaluating, Analyzing Text, is a way to involve all students in cooperative learning where each student has a particular role and responsibility to the group. It began as a way to ensure that students were reading and thinking about the text and has grown into a way of teaching (Levin, 2005).

The class is divided into groups of four to six students, with one student from each group assigned to be a facilitator. All students are responsible for reading the assigned text and coming to class prepared to have a group discussion. The facilitator creates and brings to class a Discussion Guide that highlights major points and lists at least five questions for the group to discuss. Each of those questions is answered by the facilitator in her or his Book Discussion Guide. The facilitator gives a copy of the guide to each participant in the group. Each participant comes to the discussion with a double-entry journal that has a response on the left side of the paper and room for the facilitator to respond to the comments on the right side of the paper. Each group has its own discussion, with the teacher acting as an observer or participant, participating only when questions arise or issues need to be addressed. It works well because all students must be prepared; if they are not, the group cannot proceed, so there is a level of peer pressure at work. Another interesting outcome of this strategy is that many students who are normally very quiet in group discussions are able to contribute in their small group with ease. After the groups have met and completed their discussions, there is a large-group discussion in which each facilitator offers insight into the discussions of the small group. Often when students who are usually quiet in a group speak in their small group and are validated by the members, they feel more comfortable sharing their comments in a large group. The whole class participates in this large-group discussion of the topic.

Students need to understand their roles and responsibilities in all of their activities. For G.R.E.A.T. Clubs, keep in mind the following tips (Asbury, 2004):

- Everyone must read the text before they come to class.
- Everyone must bring the book.
- Everyone makes notes beforehand so that they are ready to share, highlight, and write notes in the book.
- Students provide page numbers when bringing out points in the text.
- Students must be willing to share and to listen.
- Students must discuss the practical application of text material.
- Everyone must be allowed an equal opportunity to participate (go around the circle) and to feel comfortable in the group.
- Facilitator is responsible for taking notes before coming to the group.

- Everyone must be allowed to share personal examples or experiences as well as opinions.
- Students must be able to relate text to real-life examples.
- Students must focus and stay on topic.
- Facilitator must give a quick summary of the chapter before sharing.
- Participants must discuss common points of interest.
- Facilitator asks open-ended questions to discuss key points such as "Do you agree/disagree? Why?"
- Facilitator distributes copies of the discussion guide to each participant.
- Facilitator asks if everyone understood what was covered in the chapter.

Response Journals

Response journals help students incorporate literacy across the curriculum. A response journal is a notebook that students use for thinking and writing about what they have read. In their journals, they share their reactions, ask questions, and sometimes respond to prompts from the teacher. Response journals provide students with an opportunity to think about a particular topic and respond appropriately. The student does not have to agree or disagree with the subject matter; he or she simply has to voice an opinion and react to the content area material. Response journals can be a very effective way to assess students' comprehension.

Some teachers use response journals as a way to let students write in streams of consciousness without concern for spelling, grammar, and mechanics of writing. Other teachers see response journals as an opportunity for students to write, think, and respond to text in a way that reflects their knowledge of content and to show their ability to write a cohesive paragraph.

Self-Questioning

Asking questions throughout the reading process is critical for successful content literacy. Good readers constantly ask themselves question after question as they read content. Some of the questions are simplistic, such as "What is going on here?" or "Why did they say that?" and some are more in-depth and specific, but they all lead the reader to thinking about the content and making decisions about its meaning. Struggling readers do not normally think about the content as they read. In an informal survey of college students in a remedial reading course, students were asked if they asked themselves questions and thought about the text as they read. In general, they said that they hardly ever asked questions while they were reading; most of the time, they were wondering how many more pages they had left to read or they were thinking of something entirely unrelated.

Self-questioning focuses the reader and helps to guide his or her thinking about the content. Readers should ask questions before, during, and after reading. With practice, it becomes a natural part of the reading process. For example, when you read a newspaper and the headline says "Out of Jail," you automatically ask yourself, "Who is out of jail?" As you read the article, new questions come to mind. "What was his crime? Why did he do it?" These questions help the reader develop and practice reading-comprehension skills. The handout in Model 27 helps students recognize the importance of self-questioning skills.

Anticipation Guide

Anticipation guides are an excellent way to ask students to think about a specific topic that they will be reading about (Herber, 1978). This strategy incorporates content with prior knowledge, as students are asked to agree or disagree with statements that have no right or wrong answer. Teachers create statements that challenge or support students' preconceived notions about the ideas and concepts in the text. These statements generally enhance class or small-group discussions and can be controversial. Model 28 is an example of an anticipation guide for a passage on the rights of eighteen-year-old students.

Knowledge Rating

Vocabulary in content areas can be very challenging for students. Knowledge rating was designed as an alternative to the use of a vocabulary notebook (Blachowicz & Ogle, 2001). Although notebooks can be helpful, knowledge rating keeps the vocabulary a bit more interesting. The teacher chooses several words from the content lesson. Those words are written on a knowledge rating sheet that asks students to rate their knowledge of each word according to one of the following categories: 1—Know It Well, 2—Think I Know It, 3—Have Heard It or Seen It, 4—No Clue. The class is generally broken into groups and students are asked to discuss their knowledge of each word. The teacher acts as an observer or a participant, responding to students' questions or concerns. Use these words as a starting point for a content lesson, either predicting what the lesson will be about or predicting how these words will be used. Model 29 is a sample of this format.

Save the Last Word for Me

Save the Last Word for Me is a thought-provoking and engaging strategy (Short, Harste, & Burke, 1996). Students are given several index cards and are asked to read a content selection to identify two to three sentences, paragraphs, or sections of the text that they find interesting or provocative or that they had a reaction to while they were reading. After reading, the students use the index cards to record their information. They write the quote on the front of an index card and then they write their comments and thoughts about each of the statements on the back of the card.

Students are divided into groups of four or five and each group works independently. One student begins by reading his or her quote to the group. Each member of the group is asked to comment on the student's quote; after they have all commented, the student who wrote the quote shares his or her comments with the group.

This strategy for gaining greater understanding of the text ends with a whole-class discussion comparing the quotes chosen and the reactions of the groups. The teacher should ask whether all of the conversation related to the content helped students toward a better understanding of the text.

Save the Last Word for Me provides practice with the content in an authentic situation. Students express their reactions and opinions and learn to listen to other perspectives, with the final outcome resulting in greater understanding of the content material.

The literacy strategies discussed in this chapter are just a sample of the many ways of teaching your students to monitor their comprehension during reading and to think about the content while they are reading. The strategies provide opportunities for independent learning and for large- and small-group interactions. They show students the value of preparation and the use of graphic organizers to categorize information. In essence, they offer a variety of ways that students can learn to be successful in content areas.

The way you implement these strategies is a critical component leading to the success of your students. Take the time to teach and model each of the strategies you choose to incorporate into your content program. Explain to students the ways in which these strategies can make a difference in their academic lives. Ask students to think about and reflect on how the strategies helped them in each of the activities in which they participated. The progress that you hope to see in your students' literacy across the curriculum develops over time. Vary the strategies that you teach and make sure that you bring them back again, giving your students continued guided practice. In time, your students will be able to create their own strategies and tools, which will help them navigate difficult content material.

Advice from the Field

- Remember that all teachers are reading teachers. If you want your students to understand the content, they must be able to comprehend the text. To comprehend the text, students must be strategic readers who can call on the necessary skills to better understand content area study.

- Use a variety of strategies in your classes. Students respond well to some strategies and not to others. Vary the activities that you choose and help students determine which strategies work best for them.

- Encourage students to become strategic readers by modeling what you do when you read text and write essays, science lab reports, or narrative pieces. They learn by seeing the process and trying it in a risk-free environment.

- Recognize that many of your students will not be reading on the grade level of the text being used in your content area, so you must use strategies that will help students understand the text.

- Make available a variety of reading materials (such as newspapers, magazines, books on many different levels) that will help struggling readers gain perspective and information relating to the topic they are studying.

Additional Resources

Blachowicz, C. L. Z., & Ogle, D. (2001). *Reading comprehension: Strategies for independent learners.* New York: Guilford.

Harvey, S., & Goudvis, A. (2000). *Strategies that work: Teaching comprehension to enhance understanding.* Portland, ME: Stenhouse.

Tovani, C. (2000). *I read it, but I don't get it.* Portland, ME: Stenhouse.

Zwiers, J. (2004). *Building reading comprehension habits in grade 6–12: A toolkit of classroom activities.* Newark, DE: International Reading Association.

References

Asbury, E. (2004). Handout created for the Institute for Teacher Development (I.T.D.).

Blachowicz, C. L. Z., & Obrochta, C. (2005). Vocabulary visits: Virtual field trips for content vocabulary development. *The Reading Teacher, 59,* 262–268.

Fisher, P. (2004). Vocabulary lessons. *Educational Leadership, 61*(6), 66–69.

Levin, F. (2005). Using the G.R.E.A.T. Club strategy. *New Jersey Reading Association Newsletter, 2,* Spring issue.

Herber, H. L. (1978). *Teaching reading in the content areas* (2nd ed.). Upper Saddle River, NJ: Prentice Hall.

Ogle, D., Klemp, R., & McBride, B. (2007). *Building literacy in social studies: Strategies for improving comprehension and critical thinking.* Alexandria, VA: Association for School Curriculum and Development.

Short, K. G., Harste, J. C., & Burke, C. (1996). *Creating classrooms for authors and inquirers* (2nd ed). Portsmouth, NH: Heinemann.

Wade, S. E., & Moje, E. B. (2001). The role of text in classroom learning: Beginning an online dialogue. *Reading Online, 5*(4). www.readingonline.org/articles/art_index.asp?HREF=/articles/handbook/wade/index.html

 # Online Resources

www.tea.state.tx.us/reading/practices/redbk4.pdf
www.teacher.scholastic.co/reading/bestpractices/comprehension/ strategies
www.madison.k12.wi.us/tnl/langarts/mosaic.htm
www.literacymatters.org/content/readandwrite/reading.htm
www.sarasota.k12.fl.us/sarasota/interdiscrdg.htm

Model 24

Today's Class

Three things I learned today . . .

_____

_____

I have a question about . . .

_____

_____

One important fact that I never knew . . .

_____

_____

I wonder about . . .

_____

_____

I need a little more help with . . .

_____

_____

Model 25

Graphic Organizer

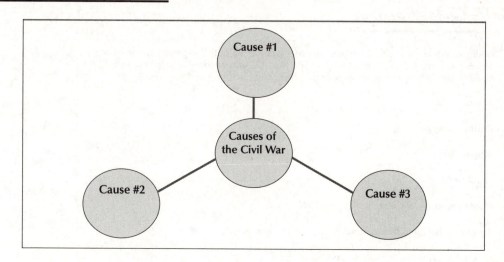

Story Map for Middle School Language Arts/ Literacy Class

Title
_____

Story
_____

Characters
_____

Problem
_____

Events
_____

_____

_____

Solution
_____

Self-Questioning

Asking questions throughout the reading process is very helpful. You should ask questions before you read, while you read, and after you read. Use this handout to help your self-questioning skills by writing down your questions before, during, and after reading.

Before reading:

During reading:

After reading:

Think about:

What questions were answered as you read?

If you went back and reread, were your questions answered?

How did self-questioning help you understand this reading?

Anticipation Guide

Directions: Before you read this selection, read the statements below and make a check in the appropriate column, indicating those with which you agree or disagree.

Agree	Disagree	
_____	_____	1. Eighteen-year-olds are too young to join the military.
_____	_____	2. Eighteen-year-olds should be allowed to vote.
_____	_____	3. Because of the accident rate, the driving age should be twenty-five.
_____	_____	4. Eighteen-year-olds should be allowed to drink, with parents' permission.

Read the selection and then discuss your answers with your small group.

Knowledge Rating Chart

Word	Know It Well (1)	Think I Know It (2)	Have Heard It or Seen It (3)	No Clue (4)
tropical storm				
radiometer				
storm surge				
meteorologist				
oceanic				

7

Helping All Students Find Success

Working with English Language Learners, Struggling Readers, Gifted Readers, and Students with Special Needs

Teachers have tremendous responsibilities in the classroom. Competence in a content area and an understanding of pedagogy are only part of the preparation for teaching. The major task that teachers must accept is to help each and every student in their classes find success—not always an easy task, even though teachers want all students to do their very best. There can be many impediments for students

to achieve success in their work. These impediments often include cultural differences, learning to speak English as English Language Learners, experiencing failure as struggling readers, or feeling different as gifted learners.

In just about every school district in this country, students from all over the world are entering classrooms. Diversity is a fact of life throughout the United States. Effective teachers understand students' diverse cultural and educational experiences and address their varied learning styles by using appropriate teaching techniques. As a new teacher, you should expect that all of your classes will consist of a diverse group of students in terms of family history, customs, culture, native language, special needs, reading ability, and intelligence levels. Teachers must acknowledge and honor the differences in students and respect their understanding of the world. Each classroom has students on varying academic levels as well as students of different cultures, and this will affect how they perform, how they interpret, and how they understand.

Approximately one in seven school-age children in the United States speaks a language at home that is not English. Almost five million students have been classified as limited English proficient (LEP) (National Center for Education Statistics, 2004). Although most of those students (75 percent) speak Spanish, many other languages are represented, including Vietnamese, Hmong, Korean, Arabic, Chinese, Russian, Portuguese, Navajo, and others (Smallwood, 2002). With those facts in mind, we begin our discussion.

Understanding Cultural Differences

Ironically, as school populations are becoming more ethnically diverse, the teaching force in the United States remains homogeneous. Research tells us that most teachers are middle-class, middle-aged, white women (National Center for Education Statistics, 2004). There is a significant need to heighten teachers' awareness and understanding of diversity in the classroom. Teachers must have a clear understanding of the impact that culture has on a person's life and consider that information in the planning and implementation of lessons.

In your role as teacher, you must be willing to learn and accommodate the various cultures represented in your class. In addition to reading and discussing multicultural literature throughout the year, you must be aware of specific features of your students' cultures that may be different from yours. Many cultures have different codes of behavior that must be respected. Teachers must be well-informed and sensitive to culture.

In certain cultures, for example, children are taught not to look at adults while they are being spoken to. If you are speaking to a student who is looking down, you may think the child is being disrespectful, but he actually may be showing you great respect. In some cultures, children are taught to be passive and not show off what they know. That may lead to a student's silence even when she comprehends what you are teaching. Understanding students' cultural backgrounds can lead to more effective teaching. Recommendations to promote cultural understanding include the following:

- Learn about students' cultures by researching cultural information. Learn about their basic culture, including food, dress, music, and so on, as well as the more meaningful aspects of the culture (child-rearing, gender roles, family values, etc.).

- Try to incorporate multicultural viewpoints into your discussions.

- Be empathetic and open-minded about cultural differences.

- Show an interest in the family and try to attend neighborhood or cultural events. This show of support will be greatly appreciated.

- Send newsletters home on a consistent basis. If the majority of your students' families speak Spanish, try to have the newsletter translated so that more parents can feel involved and understand what is going on in the classroom.

- Remain aware of your own attitudes toward various cultures.

- Demonstrate an interest and a caring attitude about your students' cultures.

What Is Cultural Diversity?

At one time, the United States was referred to as a "melting pot" because a great number of cultural groups came to the United States wanting to assimilate and become "Americanized." For many, it was important to "lose the accent" and become just like everyone else. Immigrant adults took classes in English and their halting English was their first step, their way of beginning to integrate into American society. They wanted their children to speak English, the language of "success," and often that meant not speaking their native language at home but rather practicing English. Because their children no longer had the opportunity to speak their native language, many of them lost their first language. The children who learned English quickly became their parents' teachers, helping them to construct meaningful sentences and write and correct their mispronunciations. English became the language of the home.

Today, instead of the "melting pot," we could call the United States a "salad bowl" because this country is presently made up of people from many different cultures who are tossed together, yet who want to maintain and preserve their own individual identities. In some communities, speaking English is not necessary; immigrants are surrounded by friends and neighbors who all speak their native language. Stores and businesses in their communities cater to their native language and culture, so the need or desire to learn English is not great. That becomes an issue for you as a teacher who wants to communicate regularly with your students' families. It also becomes an issue when parents are asked to become involved in their children's education. Asking parents to read to their children or review multiplication tables becomes more difficult when there is a language barrier. It is also more difficult for students whose parents cannot help them with their schoolwork.

Given the sheer numbers, it is conceivable that you have students who have just arrived in this country who speak little or no English, students who speak limited English, or students who speak several different languages. Chances are good that at least some of your students are learning English as a second language (ESL).

Teachers' views on education and students may impact student performance and student achievement. An understanding of a multicultural perspective must begin with self-inquiry. You must examine your own fundamental values and attitudes to identify your beliefs to be certain they are consistent with your classroom practices. Use Model 30 as a starting point for assessing your cultural beliefs. When you stop to think about the importance of your own cultural background, family history, and native language, you can begin to understand how important all of those issues are to your students as well.

Sometimes, unintentionally, teachers can disregard their students' cultures. In the children's book *My Name Is Maria Isabel,* by Alma Flor Ada, the main character, Maria Isabel, moves and goes to a new school. Maria Isabel had always been very proud of her names because she was named after various members of her family. Her teacher, on learning her name, says in an off-handed way, "We have other students whose names are Maria. We will call you Mary." By altering Maria Isabel's name, that teacher was very insensitive to her cultural heritage. It is important to be sensitive to the needs and understandings of your students and to carefully consider their cultural backgrounds. It is also very important to think of all students with the same high expectations. Figure 7.1 provides a suggested lesson plan for *My Name Is Maria Isabel.*

One of the first topics in psychology that preservice teachers learn is "self-fulfilling prophecy." This relates to the expectations we have for our students. If you expect excellence from students, you will likely find excellence in their work.

You must maintain high expectations for all students, being careful not to fall prey to common stereotypes. If we maintain high expectations, students will live up to those standards. If we think they cannot succeed, they will not succeed. Therefore, any preconceived notions that you may have because of your own exposure to some cultures should be carefully considered and discarded.

In a research study of teacher book clubs (Levin, 2003), twelve teachers read and discussed a variety of multicultural literature. Some of the teachers had pre-conceived notions about certain ethnicities and cultures. These beliefs clearly colored their judgment and expectations relating to their students' performance in their classes. This finding suggests that teachers have to carefully examine their own upbringing and belief systems before they can begin to understand their students' needs. It also suggests that teachers cannot make judgments about their students' success based on their own experiences with various cultures. Teachers must attempt to understand students' cultures and the uniqueness and similarities they have to others. Students must be made to feel comfortable in your classroom because they recognize that you respect them and their heritage. The literature that you read aloud and the books in your class-room library must reflect the backgrounds and interests of all of the students in your class. Students need to see themselves in the literature of the classroom to feel a part of the classroom and the society as a whole. Students must read books that focus on authentic stories about people of different cultures, books that focus on topics that are universal to all people. Literature that presents a posi-tive look at a particular culture without preaching provides students with the opportunity to see the universality of all people. Reading a text about a sibling rivalry or a coming-of-age story about characters who belong to a specific cul-tural group helps students see that certain experiences are universal, regardless of the specific culture. Students can take pride in their backgrounds but not feel so different and so far removed from their peers. Search online for suggestions for multicultural literature.

In some schools, the focus on diversity occurs at events or certain times of the year. Cultural information should be a natural part of the curriculum. In certain districts, multiculturalism consists of an evening called "Culture Night" where parents are invited to share their culture's food, display cultural items, and wear native dress to exhibit cultural pride to the school community. Although an evening of culture is a positive step, this should be just one small piece of a mul-ticultural plan for a school. February is known as Black History Month; however, black history should be taught as part of the regular curriculum throughout the year. Multiculturalism is best represented if it is incorporated into the curriculum

Figure 7.1

Lesson Plan for *My Name Is Maria Isabel* **by Alma Flor Ada (third-grade class)**

Objective	Students will be able to identify and discuss cultural references in this story. Students will identify the feelings of the main character as they participate in a book club using *My Name Is Maria Isabel.*
Materials Needed	A copy of *My Name Is Maria Isabel* for each student Reading Response Journal Chart paper
Standards Used	3.1, 3.2, 3.3 Language Arts/Literacy
Prior Knowledge	Class will discuss what it feels like to move into a new neighborhood and go to a new school. We will record on a chart feelings and concerns that a student might have on the first day of school. Would it matter that the child is of a different culture than the other children in the class?
Strategy Used	Reading Response Journals and Book Clubs Students will write in their response journals. Class will be divided into groups of five or six students. Each group will have a facilitator who will lead the discussion. Each member must participate in this group activity. Reading response journals will be used to stimulate discussion within each group.
Purpose Setting	Teacher will read the first chapter of this book aloud. Students will be looking for the feelings and concerns that were mentioned earlier and will discuss what they thought about it. Class will also discuss the cultural references made in the book and talk about whether they are important in the story (i.e., a little girl drinking coffee for breakfast).
Reading	Students will read this book silently. Each chapter will have questions to look for while reading the text. As students read, they will be writing in their double-entry response journals. They may respond to the following questions or they may consider the feelings and concerns that Maria Isabel has in each chapter: • In this chapter, how does Maria feel about her new school? • What did you notice about Maria's culture that may be the same or different from yours? • What would you have done if you were Maria?
After Reading	Students will meet in their groups and discuss *My Name Is Maria Isabel.* The facilitator will lead the discussion and be sure to include all members. The teacher will circulate and monitor the students' understanding of the book.
After Book Club	Students will create a graphic organizer that will identify the cultural references made in the text. Each group will present its graphic organizer and discuss the impact on Maria.

in a variety of natural ways, such as through read-alouds, class library materials, discussions, use of appropriate content materials, and research. Students will gain significantly greater understanding of a multicultural text if reading the text is followed by rich discussion. Students should have time to reflect, talk to their peers, write their thoughts and questions, and participate in important discussions in the classroom.

English Language Learners

How do you teach children who do not speak English when you do not speak their native language? Traditionally, bilingual programs have addressed the needs of these students, but because so many languages are now represented in the United States, it has become impossible for even multilingual teachers to be able to speak so many different languages. Therefore, it has become the responsibility of all classroom teachers to know how to teach ELLs. Even though an ELL may be pulled out of your classroom for a period or two for additional support in English, the student will be with you for the remainder of the day. An English-speaking class greatly benefits ELLs by giving them opportunities to hear and use the language in context.

Teachers must find a way to effectively address the needs of ELLs. Using a balanced literacy approach is an appropriate way to begin this discussion. Balanced literacy addresses listening, speaking, viewing, reading, and writing. Balanced literacy involves integrated lessons that emphasize reading and writing across content areas, building vocabulary, overall fluency, engagement with text matched to the reader, and extensive use of strategies. These methodologies are used for all learners; however, the unique challenges to ELLs who are also beginning readers include the following (Whalen Ariza, 2006):

- sound/symbol dissimilarity or interference

- oral language constraints

- limitations caused by lack of background knowledge

- difficulties with the structures of the text and cultural mismatches

Becoming aware of these challenges is the first step to helping the ELLs in your classroom. Your task will be to try to fill in necessary information using films, pictures, gestures, videos, peer tutoring, and help from the ESL teacher in the school.

When students in your class are beginning to learn English, there are many activities that will help them transition into speaking English, such as shared reading, language experience approach, writing, projects, and such oral language activities as discussions, literature circles, and so on. Shared reading offers students the opportunity to listen to text read aloud and to participate when possible. Other ways to help oral language fluency is to use readers theater, role-playing, skits, and rehearsed readings.

The language experience approach provides students with the time to work closely with the teacher to dictate a story in their own words and then to have that story typed and read over and over again. This strategy teaches students that you value their words, gives them practice in oral language, and provides text that they can read. Although traditionally used in elementary grades, it is a great strategy for middle and high school students and can be done with individual students or small groups. For example, students may dictate a language experience story about a field trip or film and then use that dictated text as reading material. Flash cards can be made for practice and students begin to use their own created text to help improve their reading.

English language learners need to develop an understanding of English by using English as much as possible. Teach students by modeling appropriate greetings to other students, by asking questions, by making conversation, and by using gestures. Use print to expand your students' knowledge of English by labeling items in the classroom and by carefully writing directions, schedules, and information that students must know. Use this print as you would a word wall and go over these items with your second language learners daily or until you think they understand.

English language learners must have the opportunity to practice asking and answering questions related to content, from simple yes/no questions and answers to more challenging short responses and longer, extended responses. It is important to model clear and understandable language for students while using gestures and facial expressions to help them make meaning.

English language learners must be given many opportunities for writing and reading. Providing students with a monitored sustained silent reading period offers time for ELLs to practice reading without pressure or difficult assignments. It is a way to monitor what they are reading and how they are doing with their self-selected text. Independent reading is an excellent way for students to feel like they are a part of the class, exploring books at their own pace and reading what they like. Using learning logs and journals offers valuable experience for students. For example, writing in a journal provides an excellent opportunity for teachers to respond appropriately to students' writing, suggesting word choices or rephrasing students' words to help them see how their writing can be improved easily.

Cooperative learning is an excellent strategy to use for ELLs because students may be more likely to speak to each other and learn from one another in small groups. Peer tutoring or partner work is helpful because it provides another context where English is spoken and it is student centered. Students who are paired with other students often form bonds with one another and can provide help that reaches beyond the scope of the teacher. The key is to provide a student-centered environment that offers hands-on, active learning. Direct experiences, field trips, role-playing, group projects, photographs, charts, and concrete materials help the ELL to better understand his or her surroundings.

Using technology with ELLs is often another effective way to help students learn English. Many software programs and websites are available that can make time spent on a computer very productive for ELLs. Some websites translate most languages to English, offering dictionaries in many languages. For example, www.enchantedlearning.com/dictionary.html provides definitions with the words used in meaningful sentences.

Adapting your instruction is a way to provide additional help for ELLs. Be mindful of areas in your lessons that may be challenging for your students. Vocabulary, background knowledge, and syntax are often areas that require greater practice for ELLs.

Let's look at the way you would teach a typical lesson. Normally, you begin a lesson by activating prior knowledge and discussing the topic. You may discuss the new vocabulary words within the context of a sentence or the piece you are about to assign to your students. These are elements of a good lesson that will help all students. Next, you give students a purpose for reading and then ask them to read silently for the first read. Oral reading at that point would be inappropriate because students may have pronunciation problems and would not want to read any text aloud. Being aware of specific challenges for ELLs will help to guide your teaching. After students read silently, you begin the discussion. You may ask students questions and require them to go back to the text to find the correct answer. You may do small-group discussions or a project to help students understand of the text. These are good teaching techniques for all students, but especially for those students who are ELLs.

Many educators have been taught that teaching second language learners requires just plain good teaching. However, it is far more than just good teaching. It involves understanding that ELLs need explicit opportunities to practice using their new language, believing that all children can learn, and having high expectations for all of the students in your classroom. Therefore, in addition to appropriate teaching, the following suggestions may help guide and inform your teaching of English Language Learners:

- Give students more time to complete an assignment.
- Offer challenging work, but allow extra time for practice. Always model what you want your students to do.
- Underline important directions and focus words.
- Tape-record stories so that students can listen to them several times.
- Write directions clearly and simply.
- Allow students to work with a partner or in small groups as well as individually in a nonthreatening classroom environment.
- Permit students to use computers to complete assignments.
- Allow students to tape-record their answers if writing is a more difficult process.
- Provide many opportunities for discussion.
- Use technology to help students find success.
- Teach using thematic units or inquiry-based teaching, relating the theme to real life, authentic interests and issues.
- Always build on students' strengths.

*D*ifferentiating Instruction for English Language Learners

One of the great difficulties for ELLs is that they have to learn academic English as well as master conversational English. Academic subject matter is often dense and difficult to understand. Helping students to gain further competence can be enhanced by increasing the amount of oral language in your classroom. In an elementary classroom, this may be accomplished through conversations during circle time, talking about hobbies, weather, families, sports, and other topics that arise within the context of your classroom, and by cooperative learning and partner work. In middle and high school classrooms, it is important to allow sufficient time for discussions, cooperative learning, and peer or partner work.

Use the following tips to help you teach and differentiate instruction for ELLs in academic content areas:

■ Consider the language abilities of your students and recognize the difficulty of the tasks assigned.

■ Develop your own materials that follow the subject curriculum. Rewrite content in a simpler fashion or write short summaries for them.

■ Tape-record directions or hints for successfully completing tasks.

■ Use graphic organizers and visual aids as much as possible. Discuss with students how they relate to the text.

■ Write study guides to help students understand the chapters. Gradually leave out information so that students learn to complete the study guides and eventually learn to write study guides by themselves.

■ Teach students several methods of note-taking and provide think-alouds and examples of how you would take notes on a particular chapter.

■ Provide experiences that activate prior knowledge and schemata for students, including films, read-alouds, discussions, speakers, charts, and maps.

■ Break assignments into smaller, more manageable tasks. Provide alternatives if other assignments allow students to work from positions of strength.

■ Construct assignments and projects using a specific routine that can be followed throughout the year. Students react more favorably if they know exactly what they have to do.

■ Be aware of the amount of talking you do in class. Allow sufficient wait time after you ask a question; rephrase the question, if necessary.

■ Provide ample opportunities for students to speak to one another. English language learners need considerable practice speaking to other students.

■ Use strategies that will help simplify the topic for your students. Use K-W-L charts, vocabulary charts, study techniques, and so on, to help them understand the text and the topic.

■ Try to relate what you are teaching to students' cultural backgrounds, if possible.

■ Provide hands-on materials and experiences for students.

■ Review key vocabulary and concepts in chapters on a regular basis.

Struggling Readers

What makes some students struggling readers while others who seem to be of similar intelligence good readers? Some students may have a disability that makes reading difficult to learn. Some students may not have been read to at home or given enough literacy experiences as young children that would help them to become better readers. Still others may have not had appropriate reading instruction in school. Regardless of the reasons, teachers must recognize that many students who are considered struggling readers, who are reading several years below their grade level, have already experienced failure and feelings of inadequacy. Many believe that they are unable to learn while others have shut down. What can teachers do to help struggling readers find success?

First of all, teachers must find out about their students, their interests and their difficulties in reading. Classroom assessments may provide some important information as would the help of the Reading Specialist or the Child Study Team. You must figure out the problems so you can address them. Student needs may be in phonemic awareness, phonics, comprehension, fluency, or vocabulary. Strategies and skill development for each of those areas will help students progress in literacy. If you don't know enough about teaching reading, seek out professional development or take a graduate course. In the meantime, think about what it must be like to struggle and create situations where struggling readers can succeed and feel good about their learning.

Differentiating instruction is very important for struggling readers. All students, including those who have had consistent difficulties with literacy, must be able to complete the work assigned in your classroom. Therefore, activities and assignments must be appropriately modified so that all students will be able to find success and feel comfortable in the process.

Readers need to know how to apply reading strategies and how these strategies fit into the big picture of reading. To teach appropriately, you need to know evidence-based reading strategies to help the struggling readers in your class. It is important to teach scaffolded lessons, lessons that offer the gradual release of responsibility to students. For example, teaching a lesson on previewing as a strategy for understanding a text might begin by looking at a specific book or chapter title and saying to the students (modeling), "When I look at this title, I think of . . ." The teacher then begins to formulate opinions about what the text might discuss. Look at illustrations in the text and talk to the students as you are thinking aloud about the text. Tell them you are thinking because that is what good readers do—they think about a text and try to make predictions and then read to see if they were right. Offer students the opportunity to do the same thing you just did. Encourage students to think aloud, describing their reactions and predictions.

Using effective strategies in the classroom can be a tremendous help to struggling readers. Considering the five components of reading as identified by the National Reading Panel's Report (NICHD, 2000) as a foundation, phonemic awareness, phonics, fluency, vocabulary, and comprehension should be embedded in your instruction.

Applying strategies in your classroom helps students achieve a level of success as readers and writers. Following are some modifications for struggling readers:

- Use both auditory and visual directions. Because some students are better able to process information when it is presented orally and others respond better when it is presented visually, using both modalities ensures that you will be supporting your students' strengths.

- Write directions to assignments on the chalkboard or on an overhead projector so that students who need visual cues can look at the board and read the directions as many times as they need to in order to complete the assignment. Leave the directions on the board so that students can refer to them at any time.

- Demonstrate concepts by using visual examples. After teaching or giving directions, provide your students with models or examples so that they know exactly what is expected of them.

- Allow students to choose activities when they can. If several assignments would meet the same objective, offer a choice. Students may be better able to do the assignment if they understand the format.

- Understand that students will be working at different rates. Provide enough time for all students to complete tasks. Provide additional time if needed.

- Provide additional assistance—whether with a paraprofessional, teacher, or student partner—for those students who need it.

- Offer direct, systematic instruction to struggling readers. Use strategies that will simplify the tasks and build strength in reading and writing.

Struggling readers benefit from both large- and small-group instruction, guided reading, interactive discussions, and lots of opportunities to practice strategies in authentic reading situations. Struggling readers need time and extra attention. They also require a great deal of support and understanding to help them overcome their feelings of inadequacy about school. Young children find it extremely difficult to have the sense that the other students are able to read and comprehend text when they cannot. Older students who have harbored negative feelings about reading and school for many years often give up and stop trying to learn. Their frustrations tend to lead them toward disciplinary problems. This puts the teacher in a difficult position. How do you provide support and praise to students who are so far behind the other students and may be acting out in class? You treat them with respect and you find something positive that they can do to find success. Perhaps you offer a student an audio version of a story that is being read in class before you read it to the class so that the struggling reader has a background of knowledge and can answer questions that will make him or her feel successful. You encourage his or her writing or send a note home praising something small that he or she has accomplished academically. You find a task or desirable job that would boost the student's self-esteem. You make assignments doable, you find something positive in the student's work and compliment the student and encourage him or her to succeed.

Some new teachers, especially those who have never struggled with literacy, are faced with students who, despite their teachers' best efforts, have a very difficult time reading and writing. Their weaknesses in literacy present a challenge to teachers, who must provide strategies and experiences that help students improve comprehension and find success in reading and writing. Struggling readers have a variety of issues that prevent them from being successful in literacy. Often, they have little prior knowledge that will help them to comprehend text. It is important to help those students set purposes for their reading. For example, asking a student prior to reading text to look for the reason Mr. Jones went to the farm can help focus the reader and offset the fact that he may have no prior knowledge of what a "farm" is all about. Targeting struggling readers with purpose-setting helps them to focus and to think while reading.

It is also helpful to ask students to predict and speculate about what the purpose might be. An inability to make predictions or create hypotheses based on the reading often prevents a student from thinking about the content. Teaching them to "think" while reading helps them frame their thinking around their predictions or hypotheses.

Struggling readers benefit greatly from the use of strategies in their reading. Instructional strategies provide a way for readers to recognize and paraphrase the most important concepts in the text. They are a way for readers to understand and organize information. Strategies are actually beneficial for all readers since, at times, all readers are faced with challenging text that is confusing or complex.

Students with Special Needs

Your students may not only be diverse culturally and linguistically, they may also be diverse educationally. How do you reach all of the students in your class, even those who have special needs?

First, you plan lessons that will serve students with a wide range of abilities and then recognize that you still may have to make adjustments to help those students who require additional attention. Students may have a variety of special needs. They may have learning disabilities, poor motor coordination, visual perception problems, emotional difficulties, lack of language experiences, poor reading skills, and other issues. Your task will be to teach these students, not to diagnose their problems. Of course, if you notice issues that have not been previously recognized, you should certainly contact the Child Study Team to initiate further testing for the student.

As special and general educators work together to plan collaboratively for their students, it is important to understand the need for accommodations for students with special needs. An accommodation is an adaptation or change in the way instruction is presented or in the way an assessment tool (i.e., individual and group measurement and evaluation) is administered. Instruction and assessment can be adapted or changed to help students meet the established standards, goals, objectives, and outcomes. This modification means that the standard has not been reduced or minimized in any way, but that students have been able to take an "alternate route" in meeting the standard (Mastropieri & Scruggs, 2005). This is an important feature of an accommodation—and one that needs to be consistently communicated to all who are involved: parents, teachers and students.

For students with disabilities, specific accommodations are highlighted in their individualized education plans (IEPs). Documenting the accommodations made in the classroom is essential, especially since statewide testing is now being used in many states as an exit requirement for graduation. Many states are now mandating that any accommodations requested for a student with disabilities on statewide assessments must be documented on the student's IEP and implemented during instruction prior to the statewide testing. The thinking is that the accommodation should not be a last-minute attempt to give the student strategies that will make the testing easier, but rather it should be a meaningful, purposeful strategy that the student learned and practiced in order to accomplish the same goals as other students.

Students with special needs are a very diverse group. It is not possible to approach all diversity with the same plan and strategies. However, since teachers adapt the curriculum to make it appropriate for all of the learners in their classes, there are general strategies and accommodations that can be considered for students with special needs:

- Build from your students' strengths.

- Increase the time that your students spend reading and writing.

- Model everything you want your students to do.

- Create a routine that students can depend on. They will work better if they know the routine and have had extensive experience with a task.

- Set short-term and reachable goals. Break assignments down into smaller parts.

- Make high-interest, lower-level texts available to your students.

- Offer your students choices in assignments, when possible.

- Use technology to support students. If students find writing difficult, allow them to type their papers on computers. If they don't understand a text, provide an audio copy for them to review.

- Provide explicit instruction in your classroom. Don't assume students understand. Teach using models, guided practice, and independent work.

- Use cooperative learning strategies in your class. Sometimes groups of students with varying abilities can work well together to accomplish a task or project.

- Keep directions simple and clear. Provide them visually and orally.

- Spend the first four to six weeks of school establishing a comfortable routine that students can learn. Model everything you want students to do.

- Provide written notes and outlines for chapters and texts you think may present problems for students.

- Use graphic organizers to organize information.

- Highlight important information in margins or with markers.

- Break lessons down into smaller segments. Begin with the concrete and move to the abstract.

- Allow the use of tape recorders or other assistive technology to simplify assignments.

- Repeat directions several times and in several different ways (board, notes, orally, etc.).

- Think of alternatives for written assignments.

- Test students orally when appropriate.

- Provide additional time to complete an assignment or test, when needed.

- Provide students with a model of the finished product they are to produce. This can be a critical element in the success of students.

- Offer one-minute and five-minute reminders to students who have difficulty transitioning to the next lesson or activity.
- Provide daily or weekly reporting to parents.
- Be aware of the visual distractions in the classroom.
- Be sure that you ask students to do a few tasks each day that they can do without your support. Help them to feel good about themselves.
- Encourage the use of technology like iPods, iPads, or podcasts to assist students.

Advice from the Field

- Think of your classroom as an opportunity to experience a microcosm of society. There are many differences among us; yet there are some universal ties that bind us together.
- Learn about the cultures of your students. Research cultural values, family structures, and the role of education in the culture. It will help you to better understand your students.
- Respect students' native language and encourage them to become bilingual. Proficiency in more than one language should be valued in the classroom.
- Vary the ways in which you group students. Some groups may consist of students on similar reading levels, while other groups can be formed randomly. Students can feel stigmatized by ability grouping.
- An environment that allows students to take risks and to make mistakes will foster significant learning.
- Don't give up on any student because you're not seeing improvement. Sometimes it takes time and patience as well as creativity and flexibility for changes to be visible.

Additional Resources

Armstrong, T. (2003). *The multiple intelligences of reading and writing.* Alexandria, VA: Association for Supervision and Curriculum Development.

Norton, D. E. (2005). *Multicultural children's literature: Through the eyes of many children.* Upper Saddle River, NJ: Pearson Education.

References

Ada, A. F. (1995). *My name is Maria Isabel.* Illustrated by K. D. Thompson. New York: Aladdin Paperbacks.

Henry, L. (2006). Searching for an answer: The critical role of new literacies while reading on the Internet. *The Reading Teacher, 59*(7).

Levin, F. (2003). Pitfalls and potential: Multicultural literature and study groups. In A. I. Willis, G. E. Garcia, R. Barrera, & V. J. Harris (Eds.), *Multicultural issues in literacy: Research and practice.* Mahwah, NJ: Lawrence Erlbaum.

Mastropieri, M., & Scruggs, T. E. (2005). *The inclusive classroom: Strategies for effective instruction.* Upper Saddle River: Pearson Education.

National Center for Education Statistics. (2004). *Mini-digest of education statistics 2003.* Washington, DC: U.S. Department of Education.

National Institute of Child Health and Human Development. (2000). Report of the National Reading Panel. *Teaching children to read: An evidence-based assessment of the scientific research literature on reading and its implications for reading instruction.* (NIH Publication No. 00-4769). Washington, DC: Government Printing Office.

Smallwood, B. (2002). *Thematic literature and curriculum for English language learners in early childhood education.* Washington, DC: ERIC Clearinghouse on Languages and Linguistics. (ERIC Digest EDO-FL-02-08).

Snow, C. E., Burns, S. E., & Griffin, P. (Eds.). (1998). *Preventing reading difficulties in young children.* Washington, DC: National Academy Press.

Whalen Ariza, E. (2006). *Not for ESOL teachers: What every classroom teacher needs to know about the linguistically, culturally, and ethnically diverse student.* Boston: Pearson Education.

Online Resources

www.lib.msu.edu/corby/education/multicultural
www.ed.gov/offices/OBSERS/IDEA/updates.html
www.nichey.org/index.html
www.ourkids.org/
www.multiculturalchildrenslit.com

Cultural Beliefs Assessment

Teachers must look at their own cultural beliefs in order to gain a broader under-standing of the other cultures represented in their classes. Consider the following questions related to your culture and family:

1. What is your family's nationality?

2. Why did your ancestors come to the United States?

3. What would you say are the most important beliefs in your cultural community?

4. Does your family have special traditions? Are they consistent with your cultural traditions?

5. How important is receiving an education—high school? college? graduate school?—in your culture?

6. Who are the decision makers in your family? Is this traditional for your cultural community?

7. Do you believe that respect is an important part of your cultural traditions? If so, in what way?

8. Are there traditions in your culture that are different from those of what you see as the average American family?

9. Does your family have values or beliefs that are consistent with your cultural community?

10. How important are names in your culture?

11. How would you characterize the treatment of children in your cultural community?

12. Is there anything you would need to explain to a teacher about your culture to make her or him sensitive to the traditions of your culture?

Using Technology to Support Literacy Instruction: Getting Started

 ## Why Integrate Literacy Teaching and Technology?

There are multiple reasons why it is important for technology to be integrated into the literacy curriculum, starting in the early grades. The most compelling reason is the connection between literacy and our mission as educators. It is the primary

job of teachers in today's schools to empower their students with the skills and concepts they will need to meet success in their classes and in their professional and personal lives once their formal schooling is completed. Because today's world is increasingly becoming computer dependent, it is incumbent upon teachers to prepare their students with an academic program that integrates technology and literacy in a meaningful way. Other than state mandates, a more immediate reason for incorporating technology in the literacy curriculum is that it allows teachers to efficiently differentiate instruction by strategically aligning tutorials and programs to individual student interests and needs as opposed to whole-class lessons that rarely meet the needs and/or interests of *all* of the students in the class at the same time. A final argument for integrating technology is that it engages students with interesting and motivating activities that require their active participation in their own learning.

Unfortunately, a problem that many new teachers face is that their technological expertise is limited to emails and basic Web searches. For them, the idea of incorporating technology into their curriculum is seen as a daunting and quite often debilitating task. If you find yourself in this group, the place to begin is by meeting with your subject supervisor and/or the technology specialist in your building to see what equipment and technical support is available to you. You also need to get copies of any software, already purchased for your grade level, for you to review. It is also a good idea to set up a regularly scheduled meeting time with the technology specialist so you can begin to expand your own awareness, knowledge, and technological capabilities.

However, while you are becoming more techno-savvy, there are activities that you can immediately incorporate into your lesson plans. For example, there is a wide range of interactive CD-Rom tutorials in all the content areas that give students an opportunity to practice thinking and responding, while reinforcing the skills and concepts being taught in your class. Also available are instructional games and simulations that require students to deal critically with real-life situations without having to suffer the consequences of their choices. Your students will find these games and simulations fun as well as academically challenging. Your supervisor and/or technology specialist should be able to provide you with catalogs and assistance in selecting appropriate software. *It is important that before you use any software in your classes that you get it approved in writing.*

Something else you could immediately do is take advantage of the Internet. There are hundreds of free sites that you can go to to support both your teaching and your students' learning. However, before doing so, you should make yourself aware of policies concerning Internet use as well as effective measures you need to take to ensure the safety of your students while on the Internet.

Policies for Internet Use

Copyright and Fair Use Guidelines

Fair Use Guidelines for Educational Multimedia clarify for educators, scholars, and students the conditions under which copyrighted works may be used without securing permission. The fair use of educational multimedia is a legal principle that has been amended to the Copyright Act of 1976 and codified at 17 U.S.C. Simply put, educators and students may incorporate portions of copyrighted works in their projects and presentations without securing permission as long as the products are nonprofit-making, have educational purposes, and adhere to the following limitations:

motion media: 10% or 3 minutes

text material: up to 10% or 1,000 words

music lyrics and music video: up to 10% but no more than 30 seconds

illustrations and photographs: may be used in their entirety but no more than five images by an artist or photographer

Students should be made aware of these limitations before they begin their first media project and/or assignment. The full text of these guidelines may be downloaded at www.adec.edu/admin/papers/fair10-17.html. Students should also be advised that although it may not be indicated on the site, all work posted on the Internet is the intellectual property of the author and/or host of the site; therefore, unless otherwise stipulated, they should treat all materials downloaded from the Internet as copyrighted.

Plagiarism Policy

Because text (print and nonprint) posted on the Internet is recognized as the intellectual property of the author and/or website, the issue of plagiarism should be treated in the same way as it is treated with traditional texts. All information taken from a source, even if it is paraphrased or cut and pasted from a number of sources, must be credited to the source.

Ensuring Student Safety on the Internet

Blocking and Filtering

Blocking (preventing access based on Internet address) and filtering (preventing access based on content) are methods used by parents and educators to protect students from viewing inappropriate material on websites. It is the responsibility of the information technology specialist in your school to identify and install the appropriate blocks and filters on your classroom computers. Having said that, it is your responsibility to check to ensure they are in place *before* you give your students access to the computers. It is also your responsibility to monitor students while working on the computers to ensure they are not inadvertently exposed to harmful or inappropriate websites.

Protecting Students' Privacy

It is important that you protect the privacy of your students when they are working online. Make it clear to them that they should *never* give out personal information (last names, home addresses, email addresses, Social Security numbers, etc.) for any reason when working on a class assignment. For more detailed information regarding safety guidelines see the Children's Internet Protection Act, 20 U.S.C. at www.ntia.doc.gov and the Children's Online Privacy Act of 1998, 15 U.S.C. at www.ftc.gov/ogc/coppa1.htm.

Managing Digital Instruction

Technology, like all other aspects of teaching, needs to be strategically managed in order to maximize instructional effectiveness and maintain classroom decorum. Here are some helpful hints that will allow you to accomplish both:

1. Immediately make it clear to the students, regardless of age, that the technology they will be using is intended to support literacy instruction, not replace it.

2. Tie *all* digital activities to instructional goals and objectives. These connections should be made clear before the activity begins. Students will not value what they are doing unless they understand the value of *why* they are doing it.

3. Provide readers with printed instructions that include the goals and objectives of the activity. Having the instructions in front of them will cut down on the number of unnecessary questions that can create chaos within nanoseconds.

4. Make sure the equipment and programs are working properly *before* the activity begins.

5. Create a protocol for digital activities. The protocol should be printed and displayed so there are no misunderstandings as to how students should proceed during digital time. Your protocol should include but not be limited to:

   a. When students will be working on the computers.
   b. If there are fewer students than computers, how much time each student will be allotted, a clarification of the rotation of the work stations, and the procedure for students to exchange places. It's a good idea to have a time keeper to provide students with a five-minute warning that their time is almost up.
   c. A clarification of what students should do in the event that they were unable to complete their assignments within the allotted time.
   d. Instructions for what to do with completed work.
   e. Instructions for what to do in the event of a problem. A better alternative to panicking and calling out your name for help is to provide them with two cards, a red one, indicating a problem with the equipment, and a blue one, indicating a problem with the assignment.
   f. Behavioral expectations and consequences for not meeting expectations.

6. Model equipment and programs that are new to the students. This can be done in a variety of ways: whole-class demonstrations, teacher-led small-group demonstrations, small-group demonstrations led by students who have expertise and/or who have been trained in advance, or one-on-one demonstrations. *Note:* It is not enough to just show students how to use equipment and software. They need to be able to *show* you that they know how to navigate programs before they are allowed to work independently.

7. Include questions on an interest survey which could be administered at the beginning of the year that will inform you of student capabilities. This will help you identify students who will need assistance as well those you can call on to be your student lab assistants.

8. Have a way of assessing and evaluating student work. Students want and need feedback on their work. Assessments should include an evaluation of their lab time and the products they produce during their lab time. (See Authentic Assessments, p. 80.)

Always remember, the key to good classroom discipline is (1) having students actively engaged in work *they* see as meaningful and stimulating, and (2) providing students with a *clear* understanding of what they need to do, why they need to do it, how they need to do it, and what they need to do in the event of a problem.

Create Your Own Classroom Website

A fun and pragmatic way to integrate technology into your program is to create a website for your class. It's actually quite simple to do. Websites such as www.weebly.com and www.google.sites.com are free and provide clear step-by-step directions for setting up your site. Once established, you can use your website to communicate with parents and students, post student work (with permission), list upcoming events, post assignments, and so on. It's a wonderful vehicle for sharing information and for keeping everyone (parents, students, colleagues, administrators) informed about the exciting things happening in your classroom. *Note:* Before launching your website, it's important to have it approved in writing by your supervisor or building administrator.

 *I*nternet Sites to Support Literacy Instruction (K–5)

A sampling of the sites and activities that you can easily and immediately use to support your literacy instruction can be found in Table 8.1.

These are just a few of the hundreds of sites that are available for your use. You just need to spend some time talking to colleagues, surfing the Web, and thinking about how you can use the Internet to make your lessons more accessible, more dynamic, and ultimately more satisfying for you and your students.

Integrating Technology and Literacy Instruction (6–12)

By the time most students reach middle school, they have already spent innumerable hours on computers, playing games, emailing, and surfing the Web. This is an advantage for middle and high school teachers, who will quickly find that strategically implemented computer applications will effortlessly engage their students in meaningful work, primarily because they are being asked to use technology they already understand. Also important to note is that post-elementary literacy instruction, unlike skill instruction in the earlier years, is typically done in a more integrated way. The most effective assignments require students to critically read,

Table 8.1

Literacy Skill	Site	Activities
Reading		
Decoding	www.readingrockets.org	Reading readiness activities, letter recognitions, e-books
	www.starfall.com	
	www.abc-match.com	
Phonics	www.abcfastphonics.com	Practice word sounds
	http://pbskids.org/lions/	Play phonic skill games
	http://meddybemps.com/letterary/index.html	Interactive phonics activities
Fluency	www.voki.com	Create animated talking characters (multiple languages)
	www.bookpop.com	Read along with animated text
	www.talkingpets.org	Text-to-speech
	www.shidonni.com	Student drawings come to life (talking, dancing, playing)
Guided Reading	www.bedtime-story.com	Read and listen to stories
	www.webpop.com	Read and respond to stories, print books
Independent Reading	www.drscavanaugh.org/ebooks	Read and respond to books online
	www.storyplace.org	Read and listen to stories, interactive activities (English and Spanish)
	www.magickeys.com/books	Read books independently
Comprehension and Critical Thinking	http://interactivities.mped.org/view_interactive.aspx?id=127&tit=	Create organizational webs (cluster, cause & effect, hierarchy)
	www.eduplace.com/graphicorganizers/pdf	Create graphic organizers
	www.abcteach.com/reading/storygrammar.htm	Create story grammars
	www.palmbeachk12.fl.us	
	http://old.escambia.k12.fl.us/schscnts/brobm/te…	Create summaries of texts
	www.kizoa.com	Create slide shows
	www.voicethread.com	Talk about and share images, documents, etc.

(Continued)

Table 8.1, *Continued*

Literacy Skill	Site	Activities
Vocabulary Development	www.wordle.net	Create "word clouds"
	www.vocabulary.com/wordcity.html	Develop and practice new vocabulary words
	www.readwritethink.org/constructaword.com	Construct new words
	www.puzzlemaker.school.discovery.com	Create crossword puzzles
	www.bbc.co.uk/skillwise	Practice prefixes, suffixes, roots, letter patterns
	www.funbrain.com or www.spellingbee.com	Play spelling games
Writing	www.readwritethink.org	Create newspapers, brochures, flyers, booklets
	www.storybird.com	Create stories with text and pictures
	www.glogster.edu.com	Create interactive posters
	www.kerpoof.com	Create storybooks, paintings

analyze, and respond in some way. The computer is an ideal tool to support this type of skill integration. Just like for K–5 teachers, there are several programs that are academically effective and easily implemented by simply following the directions that accompany the program:

- The *word processing application* allows students to compose and critically edit text with relative ease. The editing features literally take the labor out of rewriting by allowing students to move, add, delete, and spell-check with a click, thus simplifying the writing process and making it more likely that students will actually spend more time thinking about and improving their writing.

- *E-notebooks* can set up as separate folders where students can store their class notes or post sample paragraphs, model essays, graphic organizers, transitions, and vocabulary lists for easy access when composing.

- *E-portfolios*, set up as separate folders, give students a place to store representative pieces of their writing so they (and you) can easily track their progress.

- *www.google.docs.com* is an application that allows students to collaborate, create, edit, and share documents, spreadsheets, and presentations from any browser, allowing groups of students to work on projects or respond to each other's writing outside the classroom at the same time from multiple locations. An added benefit to using this application is that it teaches students to work collaboratively, a skill they will need for future jobs in business and industry.

- *www.googleblogger.com* is an application that students can use in a variety of ways. For example, they could use their individual blogs (web log) as an online journal where they could respond to their readings or to a given topic, or they could allow other members in the class to have access to their blog so they could respond to each other's comments, or students could be assigned characters and be asked to respond as they think their characters would, like a threaded discussion. The possibilities are endless.

Note: To protect your students' privacy, it is important for you to limit the access to google.docs and googleblogger applications to only the students in your class and yourself. Directions for how to do this are provided at both sites.

- *www.actden.com* is a step-by-step tutorial application that literally walks students through the process of developing creative PowerPoint presentations. These presentations are a fun way for students to critically evaluate and organize, and present their ideas. For presentation and design tips, see:
  www.presentationzen.com
  http://blog.duarte.com/category/design
  www.beyondbulletpoints.com/blog/

- *Social networks like Twitter and Facebook* can be used as research tools for students. For example, students can easily access public opinion on a given topic for analysis, conduct their own public opinion poll, or communicate directly with authors, business people, politicians, or celebrities to garner information or to do a comparative analysis.

This is just a beginning. Once you see how much more interesting and engaging technology makes your teaching, you may find yourself out of control, branching out into wikis and whiteboards and making your own webcasts. If this happens, just go with it and have fun. You can be sure your students will.

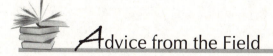

*A*dvice from the Field

- Don't pretend to be an expert. Let students know that you are also learning. They'll appreciate the honesty and be more supportive of your efforts.

- Call on students with computer expertise to be group leaders, who can help students who are less skilled.

- *Always* check the computers and software the day before your lesson to ensure everything is working.

- If the day's lesson is computer-based, always have a Plan B.

- Have the building technical support number on your speed dial.

- Invite knowledgeable students, parents, colleagues, and/or members of the community into your class as tech guest presenters.

- Become "best friends" with the techies in the school.

- Keep building your resources. Set aside one hour every week to surf the Web for new sites.

Additional Resources

Anderson, R. S., Grant, M. M., & Speck, B. W. (2008). *Technology to teach literacy: A resource for K–8 teachers.* Upper Saddle River, NJ: Pearson/Merrill Prentice Hall.

Brozo, W. G., & Puckett, K. (2008). *Supporting content area literacy with technology: Meeting the needs of diverse learners.* Boston: Pearson/Allyn & Bacon.

Stephens, L. C., & Ballast, K. H. (2011). *Using technology to improve adolescent writing: Digital make-overs for writing lessons.* Boston: Pearson.

Tomei, L. A. (2003). *Challenges of teaching with technology across the curriculum: Issues and solutions.* London: IRM Press.

Wasburn-Moses, L. W. (September 2006). 25 best Internet sources for teaching reading. *The Reading Teacher, 60*(1), 70–75.

Online Resources

www.commonsensemedia.org
www.classroom20.com
www.google.com/apps/
www.elearnmag.org

The Home-School Connection

The research on parental involvement clearly demonstrates that students benefit greatly from adult participation in their school work (Cotton & Wikelund, 2001). The more involved parents are in their children's learning, the greater the children's achievement in school. There are strong indications that the most effective forms of parental involvement are those in which parents work closely with their children on various activities related to learning. For example, reading to children, helping children with homework, talking to teachers about instructional practices that

would help their children at home and supporting the work done in the classroom all yield significant results.

Although parents are generally more involved at the preschool and primary grade levels than at the secondary level, it is important to note that parental participation is very beneficial in promoting positive achievement and outcomes at all levels. Parental involvement at the secondary level may include monitoring homework, regular communication with the school, attendance at school functions, and helping students to make post-secondary plans while preschool and elementary involvement is much more hands-on, including, of course, reading to children.

We know that many parents begin reading to their children at birth and continue with routines that are consistent and enjoyable for their children. They talk to their children; they engage them with questions and ask their opinions about a variety of topics. They provide experiences and discuss them so their children begin to believe in their ability to communicate and learn. They are involved as their children grow and as their learning progresses. They take an interest in the school and ask questions, offer their help, and form a partnership with the teachers. If all parents responded to their children's learning in this way, perhaps there would not be as many of the academic issues now facing our society. The need for parent involvement and a strong home-school connection is clear; the question is how we as teachers can achieve a positive and productive relationship with the parents of our students. This chapter will address the various ways in which teachers can encourage parental involvement in their classrooms.

 ## Communication with Parents

It is very important to develop a relationship with the parents of students in your classes. As stated earlier, the greater the participation of the parents, the greater the achievement of your students. Parents can make your job much easier if you both work together for the benefit of the students. Communication is the key to success in creating an environment where parents are comfortable and able to participate in home and school activities.

It is important to recognize that teachers and parents know the child in very different contexts so the information shared should be respected and accepted. Many parents believe that their major role is advocacy for their child while other parents are reluctant to express concerns, some because of their past history in school and others because, culturally, a teacher is an authority figure who should not be questioned.

The foundation for strong home-school relationships is frequent and open communication. There are strategies that teachers can consider to establish an environment that is conducive to open lines of communication. They include:

- Positive communications with parents, such as letters of introduction in the beginning of the school year.
- Meeting with parents and keeping an open door policy.
- Listening to parents' concerns and suggestions with respect.
- Building mutual trust.

The first communication that you have with parents should be positive, upbeat, and informative. It should provide the sense that you care about their child and are very interested in working with the student and the family. It should explain your interest in your students and offer some information on what students will be working on during the school year. It shouldn't be a very long letter, no more than one page since we want to keep the parents' interest and give them just enough information so they understand the goals, and also understand the importance of becoming involved family members.

The welcome letter may offer suggestions to parents for how they can best help their children and provide information so they can call you or email you. It's not a great idea to give parents your home phone number; however, offer them the school phone number and tell them when they might expect a phone call back. Provide them with your email address and if they email you, email them back in a timely fashion.

Some teachers get their students' addresses in the summer and send a letter of introduction to parents and a letter of introduction to students before the school year begins. This sets the tone for a partnership that can be meaningful and productive. Figures 9.1 and 9.2 are sample letters, one for an elementary class and the other for a secondary class. If you are an experienced teacher, feel free to tell the parents how much teaching experience you have. If you are a new teacher, don't tell them you're brand new; instead, tell them how excited you are to teach their child. If you want, you can tell them where you went to school, the number of children you have, your hobbies, or any appropriate information that you would like to offer. The sample letters do not have personal information because some teachers do not feel comfortable talking about their personal lives, and that is perfectly fine. Decide what your position is and augment the letters as necessary.

The purpose of sending a letter of introduction at the start of the new year is to present yourself as a teacher who is interested in promoting positive relationships with the families of your students. It is also to offer information to parents about your expectations for the year and to provide contact information should they need to get in touch with you.

Figure 9.1

Sample Parent Letter (Elementary School)

Dear Parents:

Welcome to a new school year! I would like to take this opportunity to introduce myself to you and your family. My name is Mrs. Smith and this year I will be teaching fourth grade in Room 207. I am very excited and enthusiastic about this year since we will be working on so many wonderful projects and topics of great interest to all. Some of our learning will be focused on the history of New Jersey, multiculturalism, the study of animals, reading novels and informational text, computer research, and persuasive and journal writing.

I am extremely interested in getting to know Susan, her strengths, interests, learning style, and any challenges that she experiences. If you can provide any information that you believe may be helpful to me at any time this year, please call me at 555-2222 between the hours of 4:30 p.m.– 8:30 p.m. or email me at jsmith@ael.net and we can talk about Susan and how we can work together to help her reach her potential. I recognize how important Susan's education is to you and I will work very hard to help her in any way that I can. I believe that a strong teacher-family relationship is a key element in the success of your child. Therefore, I'd like to offer some suggestions that may help to make this an exceptional year for Susan.

- One important goal for this year will be the improvement of reading and writing skills. Please make every effort to reinforce reading at home and at school.
- Read with your child every single day. You can read to her or she can read to you.
- Be a model for your child. Let her see you reading all different types of books, newspapers, and other materials.
- Help your child develop a daily routine for homework and check homework every single night.
- Call or email me if you have any questions, concerns, or suggestions.
- Please make every effort to attend parent conferences and school functions.
- Be as active in your child's life as you can. Join us for field trips and class events.

Parent involvement is a critical element in school success. We know from research that the greater the parents' involvement in their children's school experiences, the higher the students' achievement. We welcome your presence in our classroom. If you would like to volunteer or help at certain events, please let me know.

Best wishes for a wonderful academic year filled with positive learning and wonderful experiences. I look forward to meeting you and discussing how we both can help your child during this school year.

Sincerely yours,
Mrs. Smith

Figure 9.2

Sample Letter to Parents (Secondary School)

Dear Parents:

Welcome to a new school year! I would like to take this opportunity to introduce myself to you and your family. My name is Mrs. Smith and this year I will be teaching American Studies in Room 207. There are many goals in our curriculum that are focused on learning about 19th and 20th century history and political science. We will be studying the Civil War through present-day history. Students will be responsible for writing research papers and opinion statements, participating in debates, and creating oral presentations about various topics, including current events. Our overall objective is to help your child understand this country and the world at large.

I am extremely interested in getting to know Susan, her strengths, interests, learning style, and any challenges that she experiences. If you can provide any information that you believe may be helpful to me at any time this year, please either call me at 555-2222 between the hours of 4:30 p.m.–8:30 p.m. or email me at jsmith@ael.net and we can talk about Susan and how we can work together to help her reach her potential.

I recognize how important Susan's education is to you and I will work very hard to help her in any way that I can. I believe that a strong teacher-family relationship is a key element in the success of your child. Therefore, I'd like to offer some suggestions that may help to make this an exceptional year for Susan.

- One important goal for this year will be the improvement of reading and writing skills. Please make every effort to reinforce reading at home and at school.
- Help your child develop a daily routine for homework and check homework every single night.
- Call or email me if you have any questions, concerns or suggestions.
- Please make every effort to attend parent conferences and school functions.

Parent involvement is a critical element in school success. We know from research that the greater the parents' involvement in their children's school experiences, the higher the students' achievement.

Best wishes for a wonderful academic year filled with positive learning and wonderful experiences. I look forward to meeting you and discussing how we both can help your child during this school year.

Sincerely yours,
Mrs. Smith

*B*uilding Mutual Trust

Building mutual trust with parents from the beginning of the school year helps to provide a foundation for learning throughout the year. Whether you send a letter to parents or arrange to meet them in person, it is important to make contact early and to follow up with them throughout the year.

Some teachers prefer to meet with parents early in the year to learn what parents think about their children's needs and goals for the year. If you schedule a conference in September, it is a good idea to provide a questionnaire for parents to complete so they have the opportunity to discuss their child's personal, social, emotional, and physical needs and the academic issues, strengths, or challenges that they see.

If a parent does not have command of the English language, a questionnaire will be intimidating, and the last thing you want to do is to make a family member feel uncomfortable. If an interpreter is available, use that person to gain information about the student and how the parent would like you to help his child. Also, recognize that cultural differences may prevent you from gaining the information you would like to get from the parent and if that is the case, use the conference to gain the parent's trust and to help the family feel comfortable in the school.

Keep in mind that parents are experts on their children and possess a great deal of information that teachers do not have. This information is key in building an educational program that works for all students. It is important to ask parents about their children and then listen carefully to what the parents are saying. If, for example, a parent shares with you the fact that her child has no friends, you may be able to encourage some group work that will include the child with other children who may be friendly to her. The information you receive from parents may be able to help in other ways as well. If a parent tells you that a child is spending much more time on homework than you think it requires, that offers information about the child's level of understanding in that particular subject. In other words, find whatever information will help you to help your students.

It is very important to focus on the positive rather than the negative aspects of a child's learning. Asking questions focusing on what a child can do and how he or she learns will accent the strengths and abilities of the child, rather than focus on what he or she cannot do.

Even though parents know their children better than we do, some parents are not able to voice their concerns or suggestions in a positive way. This often makes it difficult for the teacher, who does not want to support a negative discussion about the child; the teacher must maintain a positive attitude and find the pearl in the oyster.

Respect for family members is critical in this process of building relationships. Teachers must believe that parents love their children and have their best interests at heart, but oftentimes, illness, family issues, or lack of education may be a stumbling block for parents. At times, one will hear negative comments about parents and children in a faculty lounge. Try not to get caught up in that sort of behavior. First of all, discussions with parents should remain confidential and certainly all conversations about students are not to be discussed in the faculty lounge. It is unprofessional to talk about children and/or their families in front of teachers, paraprofessionals, substitute teachers, janitorial staff or office staff who may not even know the child.

Parents can become involved in their child's education in many positive ways. While some parents may read to their children on a daily basis and become very involved in assignments and projects, others may be feeling the pressures of work and home lives and may need to rely on a weekly or monthly newsletter that the teacher sends home to keep informed about the classroom happenings. Whatever the situation, it is important not be become judgmental since you probably don't know what is really going on at home.

Providing information to the family in a weekly newsletter may seem over-whelming at first, but creating a newsletter is actually quite simple once you have a format. It may be a one-page newsletter that includes what's going on in your classroom, upcoming assignments, items you need in your classroom, events, but most of all, information about the class. It is best to mention each student's name in the newsletter at least once a month. It may be, "Jared presented his report on Civil Rights and it was great" or "Jessica won the two-legged race during recess" or "Tori and Callie did an amazing job in reading this week." It's very important to parents to see their child's name in print and it's very important to the students as well. A newsletter is a way for parents to feel connected to you and to the class in general. It is empowering for a parent of a student who does not volunteer any information about his day to be able to say, "Congratulations on your reading this week" or "Tell me about that two-legged race you had at recess." It can also bring the child into a conversation with a parent that may not have occurred without the newsletter. Here are some tips for creating an interesting newsletter:

- Use the newsletter as a way to highlight the students in your class. Mention as many as you can in each newsletter.
- Use the newsletter to announce classroom, school, and community events of interest.
- Create invitations to class gatherings, parties, or other events.
- Collect newspaper or journal articles that you think may be helpful and reprint them in the newsletter.
- Write thank-you notes to families who have helped the class in some way.
- Write suggestions for ways that parents can help students at home.
- Feature children's writing or artwork in the newsletter.

Figure 9.3

Sample Newsletter

Mrs. Gray's 3rd Grade Newsletter

Thank you to all of the parents who donated their time to making scenery for our class play! The play was a great success!

Next week our class will be studying hurricanes. If you have any books or magazine articles at home about hurricanes, please send them in to class.

We will be working on fractions for the next two weeks. Please look over your child's homework every night.

Classroom News

Congratulations to **Jessica, Jared, Tori,** and **Chelsea** for their excellent oral reports on "Number the Stars." I think many more students will be reading this book in the near future.

Michele, Sam, Jake, and **Matt** did so well on their math test on Friday that we asked them to be math helpers next week. Nice work!!

Dara, Janna, Jill, Jen, and **Royce** were all fabulous Book Club Facilitators this week. They did such a good job running the discussions and getting everyone in their groups involved. What interesting conversations they had! Good job!

We finished our study of volcanos this week. The projects turned out great. We loved the drawing that **Robyn** did and the diorama that **Kim** and **Allan** did! The posters that were done by **Billy, Joey, Susan,** and **Anna** looked so professional that we said they could have been done by a printer!

A very special congratulations to **Sherry** and **Karen** and **Bobby** for the excellent work they did in their guided reading groups.

If you have any books that your children have outgrown, please donate them to the school. We could use some scraps of carpet if you have any, and some felt material.

What Can Parents Do to Help?

- Read to your child every night.
- Check on homework every night.
- Talk about the day as much as you can. Ask questions about school.
- Make sure your children send handwritten thank-you notes when they receive gifts.
- Buy books for gifts, if you can.

Here are some recently published books that your children might like to read. You can find them in the public library or at any bookstore if you want to purchase any of them.

- Arnold, Tedd. *Hi! FlyGuy*. Scholastic Publishers, 2005.
- Hopkins, Lee Bennett (Editor). *Oh No! Where Are My Pants? And Other Disasters: Poems*. HarperCollins Publishers, 2005.
- Raven, Margo Theis. *Let Them Play!* Sleeping Bear Press, 2005.
- Scieszka, Jon. *Seen Art?* The Museum of Modern Art/Viking Press, 2005.

Don't forget! We are visiting the Museum of Natural History on April 4th. If you would like to come and help us and enjoy the museum, we would love to have you. There is a wonderful exhibit on butterflies that we are anxious to see. Hope you can join us!

- Write about classroom pets, trips, and celebrations.

- Explain state or national standards or standardized testing or a topic you think may be of interest to parents.

- Write a wish list of items that parents can collect or save for class projects.

Figure 9.3 represents a sample of a simple newsletter created in Microsoft Word.

Staying Connected

It is important to stay connected to families in a variety of ways. Some school districts have programs in family involvement where teachers are required to send home a weekly folder of work and parents are required to sign them and make comments. The folder contains graded work, notices, upcoming assignments, tests scheduled for the next week, and a two-way communication form for teachers and parents. This weekly communication fosters healthy home school connections and keeps the parents well informed. Other schools give teachers time to make phone calls called "happy calls" to report on successes and positive progress. These ideas highlight the importance of staying connected to parents.

Phone calls are an effective tool for maintaining good school-home communication. Although we may frequently reach voice mail, it's important to try and reach out to talk to parents. Here are some important telephone tips:

- Make a habit of calling at least one parent per week to relay good news. Keep a record of those calls and make sure each family receives at least two "happy calls" during the school year.

- Before you call home, check and make sure that you know the parent's name. Often, parents and children have different last names.

- Be sure to keep track of all of the phone calls you make, whether they are good-news calls or bad-news calls. Record the date, reason for the call, parent's response, and outcomes.

A more traditional way of staying connected is the use of progress reports. These notices are normally sent out in the middle of a marking period to let parents know that their child is in danger of failing. Although progress reports can be an important tool for a struggling student, it is as important for a child who is excelling or improving work at the mid-point of the marking period to receive a positive progress report and to be congratulated for success. These reports are opportunities to communicate with parents and to make parents aware of their child's progress, both positive and negative. A progress report should relay information that will provide help to the parents, advising them of what their child needs to do in order to improve his or her grade and work. Follow up with a phone call home or an email to show support and interest in the student. Progress reports should present a way for students to improve, and not be simply a reporting tool.

Since technology has become such a mainstay of our lives, websites are another way to stay connected to the families of your students. Many teachers now have their own websites, which are updated weekly and provide important information for both students and parents alike. Many teachers post homework and classroom assignments, which helps students who are absent from school as well as parents who want to see what the assignment is. Some teachers post schedules for tests, reports, and classroom events. Others post extra-credit activities and links to important websites for additional information. This way of staying connected provides an easy means for families to go onto the Internet and take a peek at the events in their child's classroom.

Parent-Teacher Conferences

One of the best ways to foster positive relationships between home and school is informative, positive parent-teacher conferences. Parent-teacher conferences are designed to be an opportunity to exchange ideas about the student's activities, habits, experiences, and achievements. Recognizing that this is sometimes an anxiety-provoking experience for many parents may help teachers to structure it to be as friendly and non-intimidating as possible. Parents may not realize that this experience is as anxiety ridden for some new teachers as it is for parents. Think of it as an opportunity to talk to parents about their children in a nonthreatening way. The conference is an opportunity to get to know the child's parents in a relaxed and friendly atmosphere. It is an opportunity to hear about the child's strengths and challenges and to establish mutual goals. It should be a time to share information in an effort to help the teacher understand the child's needs.

Many elementary teachers try to create a specific environment that they believe will be conducive to good relationships between parents and teachers. For example, some teachers have background music playing, and a special table in the room with refreshments, such as homemade punch and cookies. Regardless of your specific ideas, it is important to create a comfortable and private physical environment. Always have adult-sized seating, paper and pens so parents can take notes, and an area large enough to spread the student's work out so parents can examine it.

Many teachers like to give something to the parents, such as an article on reading improvement or suggested books to read at home. They use the conference opportunity to decorate the hallway outside their classrooms with pictures of the students and/or work they have completed. This is a great time to showcase students' portfolios so parents can get a clear idea of the work their child is doing in the classroom. The conference then becomes a celebration of accomplishments. Specific areas you may wish to discuss with your child's parent relating to school performance include

- classroom activities
- assessment
- social relationships
- classroom behavior
- homework assignments
- work habits
- attitudes about school
- strengths and challenges
- samples of class work
- books and class materials

It is important to provide parents with information about your curriculum and classroom procedures. Include a list of broad academic goals for the year and a copy of your classroom rules and procedures. It is critical that you prepare a folder with samples of student work and their current grades. You must be prepared to talk and show examples of student work.

The topics you choose to discuss are the heart of the conference, but there are other areas to consider when preparing for a parent-teacher conference. The positive impression you make on parents can help you develop and nurture the partnership. Here are some tips to consider:

- Welcome parents at the door and thank them for coming.
- Always dress professionally.
- Be sure to start every conference on time.

- Prepare positive comments about their child so that it is clear that you enjoy having their child in your class.

- Listen to what the parents are saying about their child.

- Be clear that you believe in cooperation and success for their child.

- Talk about the child's strengths first.

- Discuss the student's progress in each subject area and show samples of the child's work to support your statements.

- Ask parents to share their thoughts and suggestions about the student.

- Prepare a few goals for the student and create a plan for meeting those goals. Provide any materials parents might need to implement the plan.

- Make sure parents know how to reach you if problems arise.

- Discuss the highlights of the conference and always end on a positive note.

- Walk the parents to the door and thank them for coming.

- Be sure that parents leave with ideas and a plan for their child.

- Take a few minutes to make personal notes about the conference. If you agreed to follow up on a particular issue, note it on your calendar.

It can be very frustrating for teachers to prepare for parent-teacher conferences and have very poor parental attendance. It helps if you send home personal letters to notify parents of conference dates. Some teachers ask parents to RSVP by a certain date. Other teachers will call parents who do not respond and encourage them to attend. Calling parents and telling them that you were just checking the schedule and noticed that they were not on it can help to make it easier for parents to put the conference on their calendar. Recognize that even with your best efforts, there will be parents who do not attend. Some will have work or family obligations that prevent them from coming and others will just not respond. Sometimes having a student-led conference is a way to ensure greater participation.

It may seem simple to stay connected to the parents of your students, but trust us, it is not. These are all suggestions that will help facilitate a strong partnership between schools and the home. However, we would be remiss if we made it sound as if it always works like a dream. But what if you can't get parental involvement? What else can you do? Sometimes you can get help from your school.

Schools can form partnerships with community and faith-based organizations to help people from diverse cultural backgrounds who often do not feel comfortable in schools to hold meetings outside of the school environment. Schools can create an environment that welcomes participation. Signs that warmly greet families as they enter the school, resources available in the school that are linked to social services, and a family lounge where parents can come, have a cup of coffee, and talk to each other informally all contribute to a sense of collaboration in the school environment.

Schools can also offer services for parents that will help them develop their own knowledge and skills. Offering basic adult education, English classes, job training, and parenting education courses help make parents more comfortable in the school and also make the collaboration between home and school more meaningful. Parents have greater contact with the school and also become a stakeholder in the system.

Some schools support families and students by forming partnerships with community organizations that offer services to the families. There may be partnerships with youth organizations, local businesses, public health organizations, or community groups that provide information and help to parents and students. These partnerships can create goodwill and offer helpful services previously unavailable to families.

Regardless of how the communications occur, one of the most important advantages of a closer relationship with families is the higher achievement levels of students when their families are involved in the school environment. It must begin in your classroom, with a commitment to building trust, promoting a positive relationship, and establishing regular and meaningful communication between home and school.

As a general rule, here are some tips to help you develop a plan for home-school connections:

- Think of creative ways to communicate with the parents of your students. Make use of phone calls, emails, websites, invitations, letters, newsletters, and any other form of communication that may work in your situation.

- Send home positive messages as often as you can. Make sure that you do not contact parents only when you have bad news.

- Encourage parents to volunteer both in your classroom and outside of the classroom, collecting materials, creating materials, and getting donations.

- Have students keep portfolios of their graded work and works-in-progress, so if parents would like to see their child's work, they have easy access to what the student is doing in class.

- Involve families in the evaluation of your home-school program to see if they have other suggestions for ways of including more parents in this process.

- Be aware of the cultural, ethnic and linguistic needs of the families of your students and provide access and information that will help them stay apprised of what is going on in the classroom.

- Reach out to the community for resources to strengthen your program.

- Try to accommodate parents' work schedules when you schedule programs and meetings.

- Avoid speaking to parents using educational jargon. Remember that many of them have limited experience in the educational world.

- Invite parents into your classroom to present talks or skills they may have that fit into your curriculum. They are often a great hidden resource.

 ## Standards for Home-School Connections

In 1997, the National PTA created standards for home-school programs that worked (National Coalition for Parent Involvement in Education). These standards clearly define those practices that have been shown to lead to success. Those practices include:

- *Communicating:* Regular communication between home and school is key.
- *Parenting:* Parenting skills are supported through classes or assistance.
- *Student learning:* Parents play a role in assisting student learning.
- *Volunteering:* Parents are encouraged to volunteer in the classroom and in the school.
- *Decision making and advocacy:* Parents are partners in decision making for their children.
- *Collaborating with community:* Community resources are used to strengthen the family-school connection.

What is most important in the home-school connection is the mutual trust and bond that can develop between teachers and parents. Both groups have students' best interests in mind, yet it is sometimes a challenge to make the communication a reality.

There are many ways to accomplish this task and teachers must try to find the way that works for them. If you maintain a positive attitude, provide updated information to parents, and encourage parental participation with their children, you send a very important and strong message to your community. The message is that you care about your students, their families and doing what is best for their children.

Additional Resources

Dufour, R. (2004). Leading edge: Are you looking out the window or in a mirror? *Journal of Staff Development, 25*(3).

Lightfoot, S. L. (2003). *The essential conversation: What parents and teachers can learn from each other.* New York: Random House.

References

Cotton, K., & Wikelund, K. (2001). *Parent involvement in education.* School improvement research series. Northwest Regional Educational Laboratory (6).

Epstein, J. L., Sanders, M. G., Simon, B. S., Salinas, K. C., Janson, V. R., Van Voorhis, F. L. (2002). *School, family, and community partnerships: Your handbook to action.* (2nd ed.). Thousand Oaks, CA: Corwin Press.

Jongsma, K. (2001). Literacy links between home and school. *Reading Teacher, 55,* 58–61.

Kaufman, H. O. (2001). Skills for working with all families. *Young Children, 56,* 81–83.

Martin, E. J., & Hagan-Burke, S. (2002). Establishing a home-school connection: Strengthening the partnership between families and schools. *Preventing School Failure, 46,* 62–66.

Online Resources

National Coalition for Parent Involvement in Education—www.ncpie.org
National PTA—www.pta.org

Index